The World's Most I

Anthony Carr

STARGAZER

——————————————

Predictions

&

Prophecies

*PUBLISHER'S NOTE

Anthony Carr's predictions and prophesies were written and completed by June 30, 2005.

These included "The world's first full face transplant." Conrad Black's U.S. indictment for fraud, Sylvester Stallone's making yet another Rocky and Rambo movie, Barbara Streisand's abandoning retirement to tour once more; movie "Cinderella Man," the box-office bomb, being re-released in select theatres which will eventually become a cult favorite, the completely unexpected earthquake that shook Barrie, Ontario, Canada (virtually an earthquake-free zone!) and that a newly elected Party Quebecois leader (Andre Boiclair) would rise up through the ranks to drag Canada through the "Separation" mire again.

I hope you enjoy this book and thank you for purchasing it.

Carlos Da Silva, Publisher
December 4, 2005

Cover and interior design
Justin Da Silva

STARGAZER

Predictions
And
Prophesies

A Question of Fate.
Was God a Star Traveler?
Plus: Hands of Destiny.

ANTHONY CARR

"The World' *Most Documented* Psychic!"

Limelight Entertainment Inc.
Publishing

This Book is

Dedicated to

My Daughter,

Lisa Heughan

ISBN 0-9739864-0-9

Carr, Anthony

STARGAZER
Predictions and Prophesies

Published by
Limelight Entertainment Inc.
Suite 200
300 Richmond Street West
Toronto, Ontario
M5V 1X2

Printed and Bound in Canada

Acknowledgements

My thanks go out to the following people for their excellent contributions to my book, and to my life.

Allen Spraggett (Doctor of Divinity, former religion editor of the Toronto Star, author of fourteen books on the paranormal). A genius whose knowledge is truly encyclopedic, a living walking university who has passed on his erudition to me (as much as I can absorb) and possesses the patience of Job, in forever buffeting the tidal wave of Sisyphean questions about "the meaning of life."
(Not to mention his being responsible for my very first television appearance.) For all this, I am deeply grateful.

Les Pyette (Emeritus CEO, Toronto Sun Publishing Corporation and National Post), without whose "nose for news" and special "Insight" most of my projects never would have seen the light of day. This puts him head and shoulders above the rest, for which I shall always be indebted.

To the memories of CFRB's legendary **Gordon Sinclair** (author of "The Americans"), who introduced me to radio, late Toronto Sun columnists Paul **"The Rimmer" Rimstead**, **George Cunningham-Tee** and **dear Dave Bailey** for their encouragement, support and mentorship; not to mention **Glen Woodcock** (still on the earth plane), for opening the door.

The talented **Ray Parrish** for his wondereful illustrations and editorial input.

Carola Vyhnak (Toronto Star) for having the guts to publish many of my outrageous and startling predictions beforehand — namely 9/11!

B.J. DelConte (former UPI Bureau Chief and CITY-TV talk show host), for his support.

Richard McIlveen (CFTO-TV News Producer), for allowing me to annually broadcast my New Year predictions in spite of heavy opposition from his "higher ups."

Former National Enquirer, Examiner and Globe editor **Joe Mullins** for introducing my work to the highly entertaining and often controversial world of "the tabloids," lo these many years ago.

Ben E. King (of Stand By Me" fame), for generously donating his valuable time and name to my projects and world predictions.

Kenise and **Fintan Kilbride**, respectively of Ryerson University (professor of early childhood education) and Neil McNeill High School (English and Latin), for their bulwark toleration of my interminable questions about grammar and prose. Bless you both.

Legendary **"Rompin'" Ronnie Hawkins**, who gave me my first job (as a saxophone player) and has guided me though my career with his colorful, cracker-barrel philosophies.

Jonathan Bowness (assistant editor), for his meticulous research, proof-reading and writing skills throughout the spring and summer without which this book never would have made the deadline.

Tina and **Paul Higgins**, psychics both, for their priceless annual evaluation of my long list of predictions, without whose common sense advice I would be making a bigger fool of myself than I already am.

Carlos DaSilva (President, "Limelight Entertainment Inc.), for underwriting *all* my ambitions, both financially and emotionally.

Justin DaSilva (palmistry page designer), whose diligence and excellent work greatly contributed to the success of this book.

What People Are Saying About Anthony Carr

Anthony has read for the crowned heads of Europe and Hollywood – including **Sylvester Stallone, Richard Burton, Lillian Gish, Liv Ullman, Peggy Lee, James Doohan** ("Beam me up, Scotty!"), **Gorbachev, Phyllis Diller, Queen Juliana** (of the Netherlands), **Lady Iris Mountbatten** (cousin to Queen Elizabeth), **Elke Sommer, Douglas Fairbanks, Jr., Kato Katlin** (O.J.'s houseboy), **"Shock Jock" Howard Stern, Roseanne Barr, Jon Stewart** (The Daily Show) and Academy Award winner **Glenda Jackson**, now leader of Britain's Labor Party.

"His track record for predicting major events is well-documented and truly astounding." (**Mark Bonokoski** – editor, Ottawa Sun)

"Dubbed 'the seer without peer,' Anthony Carr is the internationally acclaimed psychic-to-the-stars who foresees with chilling accuracy the events that shake and shape our world, and has often been hailed by reputable media persons as a modern day Nostradamus!" (**B.J. Del Conte** – Toronto Bureau Chief of United Press International [UPI] News Agency)

From **Tom Snyder**, with regard to one of Anthony's predictions about him on his LATE, LATE SHOW — "Mr. Carr ... from your mouth, to God's ear."

"He is this country's most published and respected psychic and palmist ..." (**Ted Woloshyn** – CFRB Radio, Toronto).

"The more bizarre Anthony's predictions, the more accurately they are fulfilled! I find him quite remarkable...."
(ENERGY – 108 (Radio) Breakfast Show with Anwar Knight).

"What is this – Anthony Carr's Psychic Line? What are you – a comedian and a Psychic?!" (**Howard Stern** – November 19, 1999).

"You're crazy! How could you know those things about me? Nobody else does!" (**Roseanne Barr** – December 14, 1999)

HERE ARE SOME OF ANTHONY'S FULFILLED PREDICTIONS FROM 2005 – AND PREVIOUS YEARS

Attack on America by Arabs! "New York will be devastated by Arabs who wear the red turban and whose emblem is the crescent moon and star" (9/11); Major advances in spinal cord research: "Dead legs will walk again"; the murder of Pope John Paul I (poisoned!); the death of Princess Grace; the Faulkland Islands War; the tragic downing of the Pan Am Flight over Lockerbie, Scotland; the last (1994) "Killer Quake" in California; the "Chunnel" between England and France; the horrific Mideast overture to Armageddon (Desert Storm); the eruption of Mt. St. Helens; the bombing of the Statue of Liberty and "The White House Dome" (Senate Building); the assassination attempt on Pope John Paul II and former U.S. President George Bush; the near death experience of Bloc Quebecois Leader Lucien Bouchard which claimed his leg; Ex Prime Minister Brian Mulroney to become the first former PM in the history of Canada to be accused of corruption and racketeering.

SEVERAL ANTHONY CARR PREDICTIONS FOR 2003 – AND BEYOND FULFILLED

San Francisco Bridge—Destroyed!
Statue of Liberty—Destroyed!
"Lady Justice" Superior Court Building—Destroyed!
All destroyed!—but *only* at the Movies!
(FROM "THE CORE," 2003)

And this 2004 prediction: "New York City swamped by a tidal wave! I 'see' flooding in New York! Fires throughout posh Beverly Hills and surrounding area! Destruction of San Francisco Bridge! Statue of Liberty! Lady Justice Superior Court Buildings! In this sense the world will be hit simultaneously by a double-whammy!" – but again, *at the movies*, from "THE DAY AFTER TOMORROW" – and aren't you glad it's happening *only* in movies... (so far)? But you might remember that a film is often a precursor to *real* world events, as well as the depiction of *reel* world events.

I have developed the unusual ability to not only predict *actual* world events well in advance of their occurrences, but also coming blockbuster movies and front page newspaper stories; specifically their images and photographs. For instance I saw the funerals of Monaco's Princess Grace (Kelly) and that of Princess Diana *in my Mind's Eye before* they appeared in newspapers worldwide! I saw "E.T., THE EXTRATERRESTRIAL," in my Mind's Eye and thought it was an actual coming world event, but it turned out to be only a movie event. Shortly after, I read the palms of the late, great actor Richard Burton. I warned him to take care:

"I see you and a red-headed woman together in a speedboat about to be dashed against jagged rocks!"...at that, Burton glanced up at his manager and asked, "Did you show him the script?" "Absolutely not," came the reply. I had correctly intuited the proposed movie ending... which they then cautiously changed.

It seems that most actors live their lives, that is to say, their preferred lives, on stage and in film, therefore many of the scenes I have described herein regarding their futures will be reflected *in the work they have done and will do in coming roles proposed to them,* as opposed to their real terrestrial lives which they, along with the rest of us, have come to know and generally despise.

I have long since arrived at the illogical but probably intuitively correct conclusion that the machinations at work in the Cosmos and in our own Psyches *are One and the Same Electrical impulse* (for want of a better word that doesn't smack of anthropomorphism or a "personal relationship with God," or some such stuff) that is utilized in movie making, television broadcasts and also in keeping our hearts beating and synapses synapsing.

My point being that even though I arrived at this conclusion circuitously, the Cosmos does not seem to differentiate between real events ...and "reel" events, which lead me to the oft-put question: "Well then, what *is* reality?" After all, if what the Source shows us in our Mind's Eye which can be from "reel" life or "real" life, then *wha-a-a-t*, pray tell – is real?

And what about when we dream? Is that the true Electrical Us, which is able to wander back and forth across the Universe throughout Space and Time, unencumbered by our physical bodies? And what if we should die in that moment of sleep? (We should be so lucky!) Would that Divine Spark ("The Soul") simply go on dreaming? Probably.

I saw in my Mind's Eye a terrible tidal wave sweep across New York City and a gigantic tornado — the biggest I have ever seen — utterly destroy Los Angeles! It seemed so real I was compelled to phone Joe Mullins, at The Globe, in Florida, and describe to him my vision. He duly received it (with his perfunctory tongue in cheek attitude), then placed it in his desk drawer of "useless information" and quickly forgot about it. When the movie "THE DAY AFTER TOMORROW" was released in May 2004, here they were, the two disaster predictions — exactly as I had seen them in my Mind's Eye. I called Mullins to remind him of the vision, just as he was preparing to release a spread of that movie's *still* pictures in the Globe - in full color — pictures of the tidal wave and giant tornado destroying New York (Manhattan) and Los Angeles, respectively.

Electrical antennae, bye-the-by, are the entire neurological system, including the Pineal gland, which acts as a movie projector and recorder of Current, Past and Future events - at least visually, and cares not whether "said events" are from real life or film life. In short, you should understand that this *is* the application of the laws pertaining to Psychic function. The subtle Electrical, Atomic and Psychic forces of Nature or, if you prefer, our Souls, are at One and is One with the Universe (though corny as it sounds), not separate.

This is the Eternal Power that simultaneously records, in our Psyche(s), all of our experiences - forever.

Any war veteran will tell you he carries with him - forever — *the horrible images and sounds* of what he experienced in battle, never being able to divest himself of the *terrible memories* until the day he dies, and perhaps not even then....

Fiction writers such as H.G. Wells and Jules Verne wrote about future events and inventions a hundred years before they became fact — submarines, planes, helicopters, trips to the moon —

although I'm sure at the time they thought their creations were strictly figments of their imaginations, mere grist for the writer's mill, without any thought that they were actually plucking from the Universe images of Future Events and machines, much in the manner Hollywood writers and movie producers do today.

In fact *today*, August 29, 2005, even as I am currently desperately writing to finish this manuscript before publication deadline, I recently saw a movie – a comedy – called "WITHOUT A PADDLE."

There is a burial scene in which the priest/minister recites the eighteenth (18th) psalm!... In all my years of attending movies (considerable – probably thousands!) and the same number of *real* (not "reel") funerals, I have never, not *ever*, heard anyone – on or off screen – invoke such an obscure psalm, except, of course by me, in a later section of this book – namely: "Was God a Star Traveller?" by which I use it to suggest that possibly "God" was and Is a galactic star-hopper. This is yet another example of celluloid synchronicity.

Whatever the Electrical process at work which allows us to "snap photo images" and "hear" *in our minds* the recorded voices, sounds and music of *present* daily life and activity on Earth, is the same element used in motion pictures, radio and television. It *is* the same Power.

All events – on stage and in life – are recorded in the Great Beyond, the Cosmic Camera, the Akashsic records or simply put, the Universe. And speaking of which, here is the latest fulfillment of my predicting a *celluloid event* – the 2005 Summer Blockbuster "War of the Worlds!" – as opposed to a *true life event* on planet Earth. (Or in this instance – *off* the planet Earth!) In 1991 here is what I predicted:...

"This is a strange vision: I see countless thousands of men, women and children – all walking across desert or plains country with arid hills in the background, toward a bizarre-looking, russet coloured craft, for want of a better description. It looks like a curling stone without a handle. On each side is a huge, round, silver-like fin or wing. It (the curling stone) stands very high up on a tripod affair, with covered or chrome-like fenders covering the top halves of the feet. <u>Interpretation</u>: Before long, I believe there will be a gathering or cultivation of a percentage of the Earth's peoples by these superior Beings who are responsible for our existence here. One reason might be for the perpetuation of the human race after the coming natural and manmade holocaust. During this same period UFOs will be sighted in great number, flying in three endless lines: one going left, one right and one straight up the middle.

"<u>Another strange vision</u>! In my mind's eye there is a figure who wears a gilded crown, or headpiece. He/She also emerges from one of the strange looking crafts. The figure holds aloft, in his right hand, something shinning or glowing, and there are four or five other "figures" standing beside and slightly behind this figure. <u>Interpretation</u>: more Star-Travelers!"

<u>World Events</u>

"It won't be long before president elect George W. Bush plunges the world into war!" and "The Mid-East will explode like a roman candle, drawing all nations ever closer to WWIII"...

These two chilling prophesies I made in 2001, and now that President Bush has indeed precipitated the overture to Armageddon, we are well on our way towards World War III. The 9-11 terrorists *must be* weeded out. There is no turning back now!

That said, I predict President George W. Bush will be re-elected then assassinated before he is thrown out of office, whichever comes first. Ditto for British Prime Minister **Tony Blair**. In the end, America, Canada and the rest of the free world will come out of this magnificently. All that's required is a little courage, calm and determination to fight when necessary and the Will to do so, for the good life always comes at a cost – the cost of sometimes putting one's self in harm's way. Persistence and determination alone are Omnipotent and will carry us through to victory in the coming tribulation.

Education will not. Hitler, the tyrant, first destroyed all educators and books. Genius will not... unrewarded genius is almost a proverb – and likewise talent. Guts, persistence and calm in the face of danger will solve and always has solved the problems of the world created by despots.

We cannot allow a bully to get the upper hand. We can't! God bless the Canadians, Americans, the British – and all our allies!... I'm old enough to remember what we were capable of – and proved! – during World War II.

But we've simply forgotten how to do it – and just how tough we *can be* when push comes to shove! And if we don't get tough soon, we *are all* going to pay an *unparalleled penalty* for refusing to see the truth! For burying our heads in the sand! Peace will come, but ultimate peace will not come until the Star-Travelers return. Then *they* will establish His throne on Earth!!!

Remember what Benjamin Franklin said during the Revolutionary war (or the War of Independence, depending on what side of the pond you were on), "We must *all* hang together or most certainly we shall all hang separately!"

God Bless,

Anthony Carr

ANTHONY CARR'S MORE RECENTLY FULFILED PREDICTIONS — AND OTHERS WHICH ARE UNFOLDING EVEN AS WE SPEAK:

"Whole face transplants and re-plants will become common place throughout the medical and cosmetic industries for people who have been seriously disfigured, i.e., faces torn off by machinery or destroyed by fire." (Prophesied *June* 2005 *for* 2006 "STARGAZER"), to wit: MDs hail first face transplant!" (Toronto Star, December 1, 2005).

Black in the red? In my Predictions for 2002, I said "former Canadian citizen **Conrad Black** - now Lord Black of Crossharbour - will rue the day he renounced his citizenship to become a peer of the realm. He'll come scurrying back like the proverbial dog with its tail between its legs, when danger threatens!" ...Now its time to pay the piper, both for his hubris and his greed, especially *if indeed the stories are true* about theft, graft and not returning money to the people - after giving his solemn word to do so. His solemn word!! In my book there is (practically) no greater sin! My father – literally on his death bed, said – and I'll never forget it... "If your word is no good, then *you're* no good!" (Prophesied June 2002, "STARGAZER"), to wit: "Black indicted on eight counts of (U.S.) fraud (Toronto Star, November 2005).

Mr. Black will lose everything - money reputation and most valuable of all - his trust... because trust, once lost, can never be regained. His wife, former Toronto Sun journalist **Barbara Amiel**, may stay by his side until the last, only because she is a Scorpio, by sun sign, and Scorpios are generally loyal to their friends - even when everyone else has abandoned them. A Scorpio's motto is, "I'm your friend through thick and thin until you cross me, and then my motto is - *two* eyes for an eye and *two* teeth for a tooth!"

*Although a tremendous earthquake will shake the city of Barrie, in Canada, damage will not be severe; however, it will lead to the discovery of multiple fault-lines in the area. *(Prophesied *June* 2005, for 2006 "STARGAZER").

*Sylvester Stallone must guard his health. *Moderation* is the key word. He'll need to conserve energy because I see him moving ahead by "leaps and bounds" — literally! New Rambo and Rocky flicks are in his future! *(Prophesied *June* 2005 *for* 2006 "STARGAZER") to wit: "Stallone to shoot parts of Rambo and Rocky VI in Toronto. (Toronto Sun, July 2005).

*Box-office boxing bomb, **Cinderella Man**, about former world heavyweight boxing champion James J. Braddock (a Canadian eh!), and starring **Russell Crowe**, will eventually become a cult favorite, such as **Casablanca, King Kong** - et al. (Prophesied *June* 2005 for 2006 "STARGAZER"), to wit: "Cinderella Man makes the rounds (– round 2!–) in select theatres!" (Toronto Star, December 1, 2005).

*Her Face Cracked the Mirror" star **Barbara Streisand**'s problems are far from over. Even though she has recently faced down a cancer scare and packed on a whopping 30 lbs to her 5 ft. 5 in. frame because of career frustrations, Babs is (unknowingly) gearing up for an extended emotional roller coaster ride when she catches actor **James Brolin**, her handsome hunk-of-the-senior-set husband, screwing around with young starlets. This sends Babs over the edge and straight to the "funny farm" for R 'n' R. When eventually released she'll embark on a successful singing and lecture tour whose subject matter is "Living Life as a Fag Hag!" Her son, **Jason Gould**, is as "gay as a goose" and I don't mean happy. (*P.S. – Babs has just announced, as I reedit this, that she is going back on tour.) Prophesied June 2005 for 2006 "STARGAZER" to wit: Barbara Streisand has just announced that she is coming out of "retirement " and going back on tour!" (Toronto Star, August 2005).

Spectre of Quebec separation to raise its ugly head again. *Prophesied June 2005 *for* 2006 "STARGAZER") to wit: "Newly elected Party Quebecois leader of the opposition Daniel Brisbois, enthuses he will lead Quebec out from the rest of Canada". (Toronto Star, November) [Let my people go! Who does he think he is – Moses? – leading his people out of Egypt?].

"During a popular Reality Show – a tragic death occurs!... I believe the death will occur on the new 'Reality Boxing' show hosted by **Sylvester 'Rocky' Stallone**. (Prophesied *June* 2004, "STARGAZER"), to wit: "NBC's Contender will fight on after boxer's suicide... Najai Turpin (competitor on 'The Contender') fatally shot himself in the head..." (February 17, 2005, Toronto Sun).

"Actor **Robert Blake** will be acquitted of murdering his gold-digger wife, Bonny Lee Bakely." (Prophesied *June* 2003, *for* 2005 "STARGAZER," and NATIONAL EXAMINER September 23/2003), to wit: "Actor Robert Blake Acquitted of His Wife's Murder" (March 29, 2005, CNN.com).

"Tidal waves (tsunamis) seen only in movies become reality! Monstrous circles of water to engulf populated cities as Earth's polarities shift" (Prophesied June 2004 *for* 2005 "STARGAZER"), to wit: "Giant tsunamis wipe out nearly entire South Asian coastal communities – including Thailand, Sri Lanka and nine other Asian and East African nations – already over tens of thousands dead, total expected to exceed one hundred thousand!" (December 28, 2005, Toronto Star).

"The Empire State Building explodes from a terrorist bomb! In a futile attempt to demoralize America, Arab terrorists, who wear the red turban and whose emblem is a 'star and crescent moon,' are responsible." Also, the Pentagon bombed!" (9-11, Prophesied, National Examiner, January 2001).

"This Pope dies before years end or very early in the new one...." (Prophesied June 2004, STARGAZER: Predictions for 2005), to wit: "Pope Dies" (March 2, 2005, Toronto Star).

"**Michael Jackson** will mirror **O.J. Simpson** – ending his career.... Money depleted, spent on payoffs and lawyers, Michael has danced his last waltz and it will take more than a moon-walk to keep him grounded." (Prophesied June 2004 *for* "STARGAZER" Predictions to wit: "Jackson Not Guilty" (June 14, 2005, CNN.com).

"Palestinian leader **Yasser Arafat** will die mysteriously...." (Prophesied June 2004 *for* 2005 "STARGAZER"), to wit: "Palestinian leader Yasser Arafat, dies of mysterious illness!" (November 10, 2004, CNN.com).

"Brian Adams trades in his guitar for a paint brush which brings him even greater success!" (Prophesied June 2004, *for* 2005 "STARGAZER") to wit: "Brian Adams demonstrates artistic bent with gallery showing in N.Y.." (March 22, 2005, Toronto Sun).

"A giant comet like 'object'–visible even by day – will appear on the horizon, heralding momentous global changes," (Prophesied August 2002, *for* 2005 "STARGAZER"), to wit: "Space Shuttle Columbia Disaster!... It streaked across the sky like a great meteorite at noontime!" (February 2, 2003, Toronto Star).

"Dr. Henry Morgentaler will one day be honored for his courageous work on behalf of all women – a woman's *right to choose!*" (Prophesied January 2005, the Andrew Krystal Show, CFRB 1010 radio, Toronto; and Les Pyette, former publisher of NATIONAL POST, TORONTO SUN newspapers; and *for* 2005 "STARGAZER"), to wit: "Western University (Ontario, Canada) will recognize women's rights advocate (abortionist) Dr. Henry Morgentaler with special honor for his courageous work in 'free choice.'" (March 24, 2005, Toronto Star).

"The College of Cardinals will elect a German Pope...." (Prophesied March 2, 2005 to Les Pyette, publisher, National Post), to wit: "Joseph Ratzinger, now a.k.a. Pope Benedict XVI, a German." (April 19, 2005, National Post).

"Osama bin Laden is most certainly not dead and will resurface periodically to *verbally* threaten the free world before he or his corpse is captured." (Prophesied January 2003 *for* 2004 "STARGAZER"), to wit: "bin Laden resurfaces with election warning!" (October 30, 2004, Toronto Globe & Mail).

"The Mideast will explode like a roman candle in 2001, drawing all nations ever closer to WWIII!" (Prophesied January 2001).

"I see raging fires around the White House in Washington D.C.!!" (Prophesied January 2001).

"Wrinkled rocker' Mick Jagger will finally receive his much coveted knighthood," (Prophesied, Toronto Sun, June 2002), to wit: "Mick Jagger was finally knighted."

"A 'miracle' will manifest at Ground Zero, New York, one last sign for all to unite in world peace before it's too late!" (Prophesied, Toronto Sun, February 2002), to wit: "The day on which all the Broadway stars, and citizens from all parts of the world, joined hands together at 'that terrible place' in a defiant show of solidarity."

"A fatal outbreak of Mad Cow disease will strike Canada and quickly spread across the country and the U.S." (Prophesied August 2002) To wit: "Man dies of variant Creutzfeldt-Jacobs disease (mad cow) in Saskatoon, Saskatchewan, Canada – and in Toronto's St. Michael's Hospital, August 2005"

"A fire will break out at the Santa Monica Pier," (Prophesied, Toronto Sun, February 2002), to wit: "Fire breaks out at Santa Monica Pier, arson suspected."

"Princess Margaret will pass on in 2002," (Prophesied, Toronto Sun, February 2002), to wit: "Princess Margaret Dies!"

"Mike Tyson has one more good fight pay day before he's through," (Prophesied, Toronto Sun, June 2002), to wit: "Tyson K.O.'d by Lennox Lewis!"

"There will be "a successful bombing of the Staten Island Ferry! New York City will be rocked by multiple disasters; riots, Earthquakes, chemical spills," (Prophesied January 2001 and August 2003), to wit: "10 die in New York Staten Island Ferry Disaster! (Toronto Star, October 16, 2003)."

"The Mighty Eagle will do battle with the cowardly snake – to victory!!! This I prophesy 100%!!!" (Prophesied January 2001).

"A terrible and certainly unexpected earthquake will hit New York City!" (Prophesied January 2001).. "There will be a terrible plane crash over New York City hundreds are killed." (Prophesied January 2001).

"During 2001, civilization will experience a vigorous return to all things cultural. A Renaissance, like a supernova that burns brightest before the end." (Prophesied January 2001).

"A horrific 1918 Spanish Flu-like virus will sweep around the world, destroying more human life than did the previous two world wars." (Possibly more Anthrax-like bacteriological weapons!) (Prophesied January 2001).

"Watch for a sign in the heavens that will shock the world! Like a bolt of lightning, perhaps in the form of a UFO – it will put the fear of God in us.... I feel a great revelation for the world, as if the entire population is coming to its collective senses and we realize we have to do something before it's too late. We'll help each other and band together for protection and for the sake of the survival of the human race. Reversal of celestial and terrestrial events and properties will reverse polarities and moralities and return us to old-fashioned values." (9-11, Prophesied, Toronto Sun, January 2001).

ANTHONY CARR'S PREDICTIONS FOR THE YEAR 2006 AND BEYOND

As I sit here, pen in hand, attempting to ponder the Imponderable, I have come to accept with calm certainty, as only a person weary of fighting against the inevitable can, that The Skein of Destiny which weaves its way through all our lives is as inescapable and unalterable as Life and Death itself. Our Fate and that of the World was written in The Sands of Time and in The Stars in Heaven long before we ever arrived and there is not one thing that any of us can do to change it.

There seems to be prevalent these days a groundswell of uneasiness felt by all the peoples of the world, especially "Baby Boomers" – the generation born of my era, roughly between 1940 and 1949. A sense of impending doom, that something bad is coming down the pike! This feeling keeps nagging at these war-time babies. (And maybe they're right!) "I was born during a war and probably will die during a war!" is the oft-repeated refrain heard these days around the world. This "ill-feeling" has been created by the transiting "bolt out of the blue planet" Uranus, leaving the sign of Aquarius where it sat comfortably for the past seven years. This produced a "feel good" period of excitement and adventure because it formed a favorable trine (a 120 degree angle to the natal Uranus in Gemini), which is where it was in 1940 to 1949 when this generation was born.

(Bye-the-by, transiting means *where the planet is moving through the Heavens now, today, and natal means whatever sign it was going through on the day that you were born – then froze – the instant the Universe snapped a picture of it — a picture attached to you for the duration of this life's experience.*)

Unfortunately the transiting Uranus of *today* has recently moved out of Aquarius and into Pisces, thus creating a square, or a 90 degree angle to the natal Uranus in Gemini which is now causing all of this personal uneasiness – not to mention all kinds of *unexpected World chaos and upset!* (giant killer tsunamis, etc). This is occurring because the delicate Electrical balance of Life in each of us and in our Solar System and Universe (and Multi-verse), right down to the cellular level of the amoeba, has been upset (to say the least); so our general "Feeling of Uneasiness" is well founded. But fear not, for this too shall pass...in about five more years.

Get ready for the new phenomenon of "Re-birth charts." You probably know your own birth sign – most people do. What you are not familiar with is who or what you were in a previous existence, that is to say, a previous existence of your Electrical Energy Field whence your *future* incarnation may be determined!

When you "gasp your last," that exact moment when "you shed this mortal coil," an astrologer can make a Re-birth chart based on the position of the planets in the heavens the *instant* you pass on, and then tell you who or what you will return as, the moment you exit then enter your new receptacle. If you return as human, you can will your estate to your Future self. If as animal, then leave your goods to the A.S.P.C.A. (American Society for the prevention of cruelty to animals) or the Canadian Humane Society. And if mineral or vegetable, perhaps you can donate to your favorite botanical or geological society. Yes! I predict Re-birth charts to be in vogue in 2006! (...Or not.)

AMERICA

President **George W. Bush** will pay a heavy karmic debt for his ineptitude – purposely staged or not – in allowing **Osama bin Laden** to elude punishment for crimes against humanity. A crime not only of the century but possibly of the millennium – and just maybe the entire history of the world! Although a nation should stand squarely behind its leader once an executive decision is made, in order to show solidarity, because certainly "a house divided must fall", I must admit my instincts about this Chief of the land tell me his psyche is seriously flawed, and sooner or later he – and all of us! – *must* pay the piper. "...Mena, mena, tekel and parsin: You have been weighed in the balances and found wanting; your kingdom shall be divided between the Medes and the Persians." (Whoever the Medes were?)

At the very outset of the war in Iraq, I suggested the astrological calculations for a quick, decisive American (and allied) victory were extremely poor. On January 15/2006, a malignant planetary alignment – which will be fully visible *only* in the Mideast – does not bode well, especially when compounded by the numerous tragic accidents U.S. forces have already suffered. (Plus, there are rumors circulating that the president started drinking again!)

Therefore I predict a miracle manifesting before the entire world will abruptly bring hostilities to a halt, lest they get out of hand. That is to say, before we wipe each other off of the face of the earth!

Osama bin Laden to be brought to New York where co-conspirators will attempt to rescue him or his remains.

A fatal or near-fatal blast goes off beside California Governor Arnold Schwarzenegger as he stands on the podium... perhaps not fatal, but people hurt and certainly shaken up.

Economically Canada and America are about to reach the saturation point of the GNP (Gross National Product) after which the market place balloon will burst leaving all in shambles! Yet products connected with "sin-tax" (not syntax) will continue to flourish: – booze, drugs, sex, gambling, movies and entertainment, in general, will continue to prosper! Major and minor Canadian cities once again become favorite movie-making centers and tax havens for the American film industry as **Governor Schwarzenegger** fails miserably to lure back and keep the film business where it originated, in Hollywood.

(Allegedly) murdered Alabama student **Natalee Holloway**'s body will be found buried in sand – face up – in Aruba. I "see" it revealed by ebb tide washing over smooth rocks!

Former U.S. First Lady **Nancy Reagan**, widow of late American President **Ronald Reagan**, will soon score one for "the gipper" in the sky.

Sidney, daughter of **O.J.Simpson**, to blow the whistle on her father for allegedly murdering her mother, Nicole Brown Simpson and friend Ronald Goldman. Her "shrink" says to put the incident behind her. (Easy for him to say!) She wants revenge on behalf of her mother because "the Juice" "took up with another woman and, in her mind's eye, he was unfaithful."

Palm Beach, Florida, is next in line for hits from king-size waves and hurricanes!... And "Palm" Beach will become just about as flat as a palm!

Bad luck and too many accidents surround U.S. troops in Iraq – and it'll get worse before it gets better. Much worse! Yet with the aid of new allies the war will turn around late next year. Even so, it will continue to spread 'til all the world is engulfed!

California's Santa Monica Pier receives extensive damage from tidal waves and fires from burst gas mains and multiple earthquakes!

I see the U.S. Presidential funeral caisson.

Since Katrina, Blues from N'Orleans will be that much better!

Through the subtle process of osmosis, socialized medicine in America becomes more popular.

The next U.S. President will be a peacekeeper (that should be peace*maker*!), but alas – too late! The damage is done, the wheels are turning....

More and more "Christian" religious figureheads to be ousted as child molesters! The largest user group of child porn! "That which was most high shall be brought most low." (Revelation)

So devastating are the troubles caused by this current U.S. administration, former President **Bill Clinton** will be asked to help soothe the troubled waters: the American people are ready to revolt!

Governor **Arnold Schwarzenegger** to be stricken by debilitating nerve disorder, which is to say, no nerve at all – when push comes to shove!

During this U.S. President's *first* election campaign in 2001, even before the votes were in, I said that, "President-elect **George W. Bush** will precipitate the overture to ARMAGEDDON!" – and so he has!!!

Air quality becomes a pandemic concern when drastic measures are taken to correct this very serious problem. As with gas and oil, giant business conglomerates figure a way to profit from the disaster. Citizens forced to wear metered oxygen tanks are charged per gasp! (Don't laugh, "many a truth has been spoken in jest!")

Tired and exhausted from tension and terror, U.S. citizens effect a great exodus North, seeking peace....

CANADA

Black in the red? In my Predictions for 2002, I said "former Canadian citizen **Conrad Black** - now Lord Black of Crossharbour - will rue the day he renounced his citizenship to become a peer of the realm. He'll come scurrying back like the proverbial dog with its tail between its legs, when danger threatens!" ...Now its time to pay the piper, both for his hubris and his greed, especially *if indeed the stories are true* about theft, graft and not returning money to the people - after giving his solemn word to do so. His solemn word!! In my book there is (practically) no greater sin! My father - literally on his death bed —said, and I'll never forget it... "If your word is no good, then *you're* no good!"

Mr. Black will lose everything - money reputation and most valuable of all - his trust... because trust, once lost, can never be regained. His wife, former Toronto Sun journalist **Barbara Amiel**, may stay by his side until the last, only because she is a Scorpio, by sun sign, and Scorpios are generally loyal to their friends - even when everyone else has abandoned them. A Scorpio's motto is, "I'm your friend through thick and thin, until you cross me, and then my motto is -*two* eyes for an eye and *two* teeth for a tooth!" (*My ex-wife stood by me through thick and thick!*)

The body of recently released child killer **Karla Homolka**, formerly married to co-child killer/rapist **Paul Bernardo**, will be found in a wooded park in British Columbia, beaten and mutilated beyond recognition. This comes as no surprise and is no more than this Judas goat deserves.

Former Canadian Prime Minister **Brian** "the chin" **Mulroney** becomes so ill that a legion of priests is necessary to hear his confession which seems to go on forever - ad infinitum et ad nauseum. However, he unexpectedly recovers and is left with egg on his face, as if to say: "Now what do I do – tell them I was delirious with fever?"

Canada must – and will – create a super army. We are going to need it!!! **George W. Bush** was elected to office and did sow the seeds of **WW III**!

Unless Canada steps up to bat to help end hostilities in the Mideast, the situation there will escalate to *beyond* cataclysmic proportions! – beyond anything we could ever imagine as being remotely controllable! *Try harder* – or else the whole world *will* burn!

Even though on the al-Qaeda hit list, Canada will *not* be attacked if for no other reason than the evil doers would lose their anonymity to move freely throughout this land as they plot their deadly plans against the south – America!

Chicken-livered Ontario Premier **Dalton McGuinty** suffers character assassination for his two-faced legislation of the repressive health tax laws against the poor people of Ontario. A law so backward that the late **Tommy Douglas**, patriarch of socialized medicine, is going rise from his grave and haunt him right into the looney bin. Shame on you, Dalton! May the fleas of a thousand camels nest in your armpits.... [Better yet — in your scrotum!.]

In Toronto, Canada, tremendous explosions level many houses and buildings in the west-central part of the downtown core. Perhaps gas, perhaps terrorists – but methinks a stray lightening bolt will be the cause!

The Canadian GNP (Gross National Product) takes off. This leads to the Canadian dollar becoming even more valuable to the Yankees. The burgeoning "Hollywood North" communities in Toronto, Vancouver and everywhere else will reap the benefits.

The next Canadian Prime Minister is a woman, wearing red, with short dark hair, who comes from the hills.

Opportunities open up for Newfoundlanders who have been severely economically hit because of draconian government restrictions on fishing. I see *new* heretofore untapped resources in the future of the "Newfies".

Unfortunately many children are killed and injured at a well-known Toronto Youth centre, as, a result of a gas explosion!

A powerful Métis leader, a former member of the RCMP (Royal Canadian Mounted Police), will rise from the west to create a new nation with a new flag.

Animal psychics become the rage! Psychic channelers for pussies and pooches interact with the psyches of pets. This helps unify animal and beast. (The latter being we!)

A string of connected police assaults on University students (especially women) will occur in the London, Ontario, Canada, area. Disturbingly high numbers of police officers involved.

When a rabid bat is discovered in Toronto, great swarms will be seen throughout the land, silhouetted against the night's full moon.

Tourists flock to Quebec City to experience the miracle, a revelation -- no less greater than t commemorated at Lourdes!

* Spectre of Quebec separation to raise its ugly head again. *Predicted in June – long before the election of Quebec's current opposition and Party Quebecois leader Brisbois.

Calgary: "Ineffable" is the only word to describe that which is indescribable – the coming success for Calgary! Money grows exponentially!!

Mayor **David Miller** is a good man and a good mayor who will prosper – and so shall we all!

Saskatchewan builds a great opera house in Regina which attracts world attention, including not only members of the British Royal Family but royalty of other stripes, including Hollywood!

The Newfoundland Board of Education to publish a compendium of "Newfie Geniuses and Pithy Sayings." (Nyuck, nyuck!)

Nova Scotia's Halifax takes extreme measures to guard against terrorist attacks when a bomb is detonated, meant for the U.S. via Boston, Mass.

Nova Scotia amalgamates with Prince Edward Island and New Brunswick and becomes a force to be reckoned with. The Great Bridge between P.E.I. and the mainland will buckle at its weakest point following an historical storm.

Vancouver, B.C.... Great numbers of unsavory people are quite literally swept away and out of drug houses with the onslaught of a tidal wave. It sweeps the lowlands and brings misery to this once quaint, quiet town. A new way to help is implemented.

"Stompin Tom" Conners retires to Charollettown, P.E.I. The new national anthem becomes "Bud the Spud".and a new flag designed whose emblem is a spud (potato) against a red background.

Ontario's Power Grids are failing drastically because of privatizing. This could put us in a deep freeze, something comparable to the Montreal disaster of   1999/2000.

Canadian Prime Minister **Paul Martin** becomes the great statesman of the world. History will be kind to him. Despite multiple scandals, Martin will win an astonishing majority government. Liberal party will win general election in 2006.

Earthquakes and giant storms wash away British Columbia's coastline! Yet these disasters are not the last to hit Canada's coast. They but signal the subtle beginnings of the strangest weather Canadians will ever see!

Some day Lake Ontario will cover Toronto as far North as the Highway 401... Some day.

*Although a tremendous earthquake will shake the city of Barrie, in Canada, damage will not be severe; however, it will lead to the discovery of multiple fault-lines in the area. *(Predicted in June 2005-long before the event!)

America is discovered placing wire taps on Canada! Unbeknownst to the Canadian government, the U.S. is keeping close tabs on Canadians long suspected of running secret training camps for home-bred terrorists!

U.S. will pressure Canada to relinquish its hold on the freshwater they so dearly covet...

WORLD EVENTS

Osama bin Laden, look at my eyes and know this: I swear by Allah and Almighty God that you will *never* see Paradise, the soft light of Heaven reserved for your innocent victims, but only the dark and stormy place at Cosmos' end where Chaos reigns.

There, shall your Sensorial Self — (your soul, should you possess one), languish in unimaginable agony until even It is finally consumed by the Eternal Fire. For you have come 'round on the Great Wheel of Life full circle, and not yet learned your lessons. And you never will. In the history of the world there has never been such a single act of utter cruelty in which so many helpless citizens were purposely murdered! Defenseless men, women and children — all. A *real* man would have attacked the military.

You are no *true* follower of Islam. However, you do bear a strong resemblance to Adolph Hitler who, no doubt would be in awe of your barbarity, were he living. I'm almost certain you *are* the Fuhrer reincarnate, with your pathological hatred of Jews and Americans. And like Hitler, you are probably a self-loathing, *closet* Jew. So why don't you do the world a big favor—and kill *yourself!* You are a mad dog and a coward. And mad dogs *must* be put down, as soon you will be. Death will come swiftly. Your suffering in *this* life will be brief, but interminable in the next.

Both Bible and Qur'an (Koran) state: "The knower knoweth," and I *know* the horror that hath no words to describe that which awaits you in the Great Beyond. This is a gift of "vision" bestowed upon one who has lived the great range of life, perhaps *too* many times.

I would *like* to believe that this "Sense of Kismet" might, in some small way, bring a degree of comfort to the grieving who have lost so many loved ones. Yet I know it cannot be...only time may ease the pain, console the inconsolable.

Remember, however, that the Paths to God are many and varied, since not all travel the familiar and worn road. But I promise this: the Fate of Osama bin Laden's Soul is sealed, as I swear the Souls of all our dearly departed are Eternally Sealed in the Great Archives of the Akashic Records of Heaven (into which Edgar Cayce occasionally peered to glimpse the future), and in what the Christian Bible calls "The Book of Life," until the Day of Judgement.

To Jews, Muslims and Christians: When Comes the Great and Glorious One *all* eyes will see *but* One, and *only* One shall rule...He, Who *is* the Light of the world. Star-Traveller or God, only He can stop the carnage. And every religion will be One.

Osama bin Laden, this you well know: "What Is Written In The Mind Of Allah (God) *Will Be* And *Must* Come To Pass." But it will not be what you expect. Should I die before this conflict is over, *in whatever manner,* take this as yet another sign of your ultimate defeat at the hands of the American Allies.

You will *never* win. *"IT IS WRITTEN."*

(P.S. There will be a *very* violent and fatal denouement to the bin Laden problem on or about February 25, 2006 or 2007.)

WORLD EVENTS

In last year's STARGAZER PREDICTIONS FOR 2005 – AND BEYOND!, I prophesied that "Earthquakes, giant storms, hurricanes and tidal waves – heretofore seen *only in movies* – will signal the beginning of the strangest weather patterns ever seen since recorded time, in Canada, America – and indeed the whole world!" Since that prophecy, the most devastating tsunami in South-East Asia, *the worst ever seen,* that killed hundreds of thousands of people and megalithic Hurricane Katrina – which utterly destroyed the city of New Orleans in the United States — is merely a dress rehearsal for what is to come! (Bible-thumpers take note: these two well-known flesh-pots, chiefly infamous for gambling, prostitution and drugs were destroyed in a fashion similar to Sodom and Gomorrah!) That said Ireland will sink! The complete Emerald Isle will be hit by a series of hurricanes, waves and vortices so humongous as to make Katrina seem like a rippling breeze across a quiet pond on a summer afternoon. A few years ago I accurately said: "Everyone will want to be Irish," what with the world tour of Michael Flately and "the Lord of the Dance." Now, the terrible storms to come (actual and political!) will cause the Irish to yearn for the "good old days" of British occupation and potato famines – Ock! — faith and begorra!

The "ELIXER OF LIFE," a gift of the Star-Travelers to the

ancient Sumerians (who called them the "Anunnak" or "Those Who Came To Earth From The Heavens!"), will one day cure cancer and other horrible diseases, will provide us with limitless new fuel sources (rendering fossil fuels obsolete) and be the anti-matter every scientist seeks to *re*-discover, allowing Mankind to conquer Space, the Infinite Universe.

This ELIXER OF LIFE variously has been called "the tincture," "the magic powder" and more commonly the "Philosopher's Stone." When rediscovered – and it exists in everything around us including the very ground we walk on – it will regenerate human DNA, thus resurrection and life eternal! – Eureka!!!

Great Britain shall reprise its role as a leader of nations. Acting as mediator between old and new superpowers, the Great Lion shall help avert global nuclear war! Watch for China, India, North Korea and the "new" Russia as major players – not to mention, of course, America. But alas, great America has "lost face" in the eyes of the world today through bad judgment, yet in time shall regain it when the *new* government becomes stabilized. (This was prophesied *before* the London Underground bombings!)

Terrible destruction at New York Airport! A blast, much loss of life, early in 2006! Also simultaneous attacks on airports in other American cities and in Canada.

Iraqi dissidents, looking to replace **Saddam Hussein,** are currently biding their time for the right moment to turn Iraq into a "superpower," of sorts, the closest the Middle-East has ever come to such an experience.

Even though Mankind receives yet one more reprieve, I see – fire! fire! fire! – throughout the Mideast and the rest of the world, confirming my worst fears and the panic gripping my heart!

A network of pseudo-Muslims attack and leave the next World Youth Day in Cologne obliterated. As a result, the spread of Christianity temporarily falters as people become disillusioned ... not to mention terrified!

Prince Charles, Heir apparent to the British throne, shall suffer loss of a child.

When **Nelson Mandella** dies, South Africa plunges once

more into war!

Yet one more fanatic rises from the East to rival **Osama bin Laden.** He wears the blue turban – a sign of the madman who will finally light the fuse that plunges our world into chaos!... (Another madman besides Bush, that is.)

Largest scam in history: gold companies fabricate huge gold deposits in hopes of increasing the value of floundering stocks.

Identity theft to become rampant as crooks learn to defraud the system. Celebrity hospital patients become prime targets when the "no-goodnicks" attempt to pass themselves off as doctors and pharmacists... Many computer deaths!

One of the Cold-Stream guards at Buckingham Palace is assassinated! It's an attempt to destroy British morale. The guilty terrorist is captured before he can commit hara-kiri!

I see the Eiffel Tower, perhaps a structure not unlike Toronto's CN Tower, utterly destroyed – toppled onto its side! This marks the beginning of the awful and terrible war!!!

Buffalo meat replaces beef as an American staple, then in Canada, followed by the rest of the world as a result of the *slow* spread of Mad Cow Disease.

A Moslem woman will give birth to a Super-Child of the World who'll possess preternatural and mystical powers.

A revelation that late American President **Lyndon B. Johnson** was involved in the assassination of **John F. Kennedy.**

Arnold Schwarzenegger fails miserably as California Governor and returns to "acting" temporarily before once again making a bid – successfully! – for the White House.

A tremendous explosion, caused by men working around the right paw of the great Sphinx! What a discovery!! A cornucopian wealth of information pertaining to our relationship with the Extraterrestrial Beings Who created us!

TV evangelist **Benny Hinn** suffers fatal heart attack during rally.

Soon – no cash. (...No Cash?! Oh, no!!) It'll be simply a matter of shinning a light on the forehead or palm to ensure – or not – one's credit line:"...also it causes all, both small and great, both rich and poor, both free and slave, to be marked on the right hand or the forehead, so that *no one can buy or sell unless he has the mark,* that is, the name of the beast or the number of its name, 666." <u>REVELATION 13:16-7</u>

Credit cards bear numbers and are generally carried in the hand and eventually could be tattooed in the palm or on the forehead! How many car license plates already bear the number 666?

Watch for the *negative* return of Libyan leader **Moammar Khadafy (Duck)**! Even as I previously predicted he would return from hiding as an American ally, he will once again flip-flop like the fish out of water he is. Unfortunately for him, this time he will flip when he should have flopped!

The Leaning Tower of Pisa topples! – (with a little help).

The Oriental horde begins its descent on the world, like a great **Red Dragon** – yet, is suddenly checked by a supernatural force!

The Hollywood and Chicago "flapper"-era returns to the world stage – big time!

Coal and peat moss come back as major fuel sources for industry.

Terrible destruction at New York Airport! A blast, much loss of life, early in 2006! Also simultaneous attacks on airports in other American cities and in Canada.

The fabled serpentine Loch Ness Monster – "Nessie" – finally rears her head for all to see!... at least the skeletal remains, which mini-sub divers discover. Once the pieces are assembled, its length will be assessed at 60-odd feet, then judged to have been a mutated eel species. But fear not, she has a mate and some progeny still kicking (or slithering?) deep down in the brine! Maybe they'll simply clone the old gal... (or lass).

Books on **WWII** and its heroes to flood global market. This ensures posterity never forgets the high cost of freedom.

Remember this if you remember nothing else: number 11/11 will be profoundly important to the survival of the peoples of the world.

Titanic II and Toronto Hydrofoil ("the Breeze") are destined for disaster – especially Titanic. Tempting mistress Fate is to court one's own demise.

Bishop Desmond Tutu in grave danger of assassination! Even though it will appear he died of natural causes (as when I accurately predicted the murder of **Pope John Paul I**), there will be no doubt after investigation that he was murdered! This begins to another bloody war in South Africa.

In 2005 and 2006 Mankind will tremble in fear; there will be unparalleled water disasters of titanic proportions such as the world has not seen since biblical times!

In the Balkans, it will be Sarajevo all over again, when a Serbian nationalist drops a bomb into the lap of a high-ranking man. This unites the *new* might of Russia as the disparate states close ranks and build strength. I see tanks – soldiers pouring across the land! Their emblem is the red star. Remember the communist dictum: "two steps forward, one step back."

This German pope's reign will be "short-lived." The next – *and last* – pontiff shall be **Peter of Rome,** who will flee the violent Turk!

Third temple to be built in Jerusalem! First more fighting (naturally). An earthquake destroys the existing structure but will be considered an "act of God" (or force majeure) by *all* concerned parties and so makes way for the new place of worship, that which is holy to both Muslims and Jews alike, and variously referred to as the Temple Mount, Mount Moriah, Dome of the Rock and the Al-Aasa Mosque. It can be built because no human hand shall have destroyed the present one.

Helium houses that float above earthquake zones to be the coming thing in Southern California; then other earthquake weary countries follow. And they are coming!

The American people will come to despise Bush even more, if that's possible! He will go down in history as the coward who precipitated WWIII, that is if anyone is left *to* record history!

Again I say, the most incredible archeological discoveries since locating King Tut's tomb! Long hidden burial chambers around the Sphinx and Pyramids to yield untold valuable information concerning Man and our relation to the heavenly Star-

Traveler – or, if you so choose – God! A sign in the heavens for *all* to see will apprise us of the imminent return of These Shinning Beings Who created us! Then peace shall reign on Earth. Until that time comes, I shall continue to predict this event every year (that I'm still around), so strongly do I feel its truth!

A desperate people are led into spiritual impoverishment. People without belief are nothing. (Remember the former U.S.S.R.?) The *pursuit* of material wealth *in and of itself* can only end in despair. (Unless, of course – you attain it!) North America, take heed!

As the great tidal wave of baby boomers slips into old age, they also become pathologically depressed as fundamental belief systems, such as Heaven and Hell, fall away. Hopes are renewed, however, by a belief in the return of the **Star-Travelers** who created us. Despair is replaced with a certainty of "life hereafter" in the Electrical Cosmos, to which the Divine Spark returns. In short, we are going home.

India's Taj Mahal will make news... Surrounded by much sadness, much grief... perhaps fire – perhaps war!

Christ of the Andes weeps!.. Leaving Christians in tears!

Within five to ten years a new world order prevails. In Canada, America around the globe the "law of the land" shall be upheld *without* use of brutal force. Those now in power who delight in Gestapo-type tactics are in for a rude awakening. Remember what happened to Hitler and Il Duce (Mussolini)? Stalin, of course, is another story. But even his brutal legacy finally ended with the "Fall of the Wall."

In 2006 Mother Church exists, yet one year hence – no more! From sea to sea, this pope will *flee*, and Rome's home no more!

The great tidal wave seen sweeping over Manhattan in the film "THE DAY AFTER TOMORROW" will be as a teardrop in a glass of water when this planet "flips its lid" (That is, its polarities). This happens approximately every 26,000 years, or so – and we are *way* overdue!

Tension between Cuba and the U.S. eases considerably as **Fidel Castro** offers an olive branch in the way of mega-musicals to tour Canada and America. Proceeds to help New Orleans and the world's starving children. Canada and the U.S. reciprocate by sending to Cuba bands with the same generous aim. In short, Cuba and the U.S to kiss and make up, with Canada acting as procurer.

The great ship is sinking by the stern... A terrible vortex – then two... Broken in half, with all its staff, evil shall be the sea where the mighty Titanic went down. Three thousand souls lost!

When U.S. forces withdraw from Iraq, Iran will strike with such force as to leave that country reeling! America and the coalition again are involved, but now there's no stopping the juggernaut... Woe unto us!

When man conquers Space and colonizes planets (as I am sure *we* were once colonized), war shall vanish from the earth – literally – for then shall there be space enough for all!

Proof positive the Soul survives death will be discovered in Pyramids— world-wide. One by one they shall give up the "ghost" (secrets), as old notions topple like ten-pins and the new religion rises.

As gasoline gougers continue their greedy stranglehold on hapless car owners, the manifestation of a new – yet old – power source is revealed, rediscovered from antediluvian times. (Before The Great Flood!!)

Australia and New Zealand are suddenly thrust centre stage! The scenario appears to be triggered by an air attack... Warships and ICBM's seem to be an issue. (I guess they would be!)

Great sinkholes simultaneously occur throughout Florida causing widespread catastrophe, loss of life and damages ranging in the billions of dollars.

Western women, now independent, make men not so eager for relationships or marriage until late thirties, even forties – hence, a drop in procreation. However, during and after WWIII women will once again hide behind their skirts while men go off to fight and die. And once again, men will be men and women, women.

Problems surrounding homosexuality will be no more. A blasé attitude to prevail, due in large part to their massive revenues generated Worldwide. This *natural* sex will assume powerful leadership positions through their wealth as once they did in days of yore, specifically during ancient Greece.

A powerful leader, such as has not been seen since "the days of ancients," shall rise up to startle the world. With **Alexander's** ferocity and **Aristotle's** wisdom, he'll lead the courageous Greek people into a great, new era.

Former Iraqi dictator **Saddam Hussein** shall be freed from prison by rebels, like Napoleon escaping Elba... but like the little Corsican, only temporarily.

Iran or Pakistan will use **Osama Bin Laden** as a bargaining chip to negotiate with the Americans.

Laws shall be enacted to protect fetuses from selfish, drugged-out mothers 'til after parturition, even to the extent of incarcerating them.

At the 2008 Summer Olympics there will be a terrorist threat –and worse! Must beef up security ten-fold. Ditto for 2006 Winter Olympics when mass riots break out after attack causes widespread panic!

Alleged wife killers **O.J. Simson** and **Robert Blake** team up to write a screen-play called: ("Who Killed Ma` Bitch?!" A comedy that becomes a smash hit on Broadway and in film – even garnering a Tony and an Oscar!

West Nile virus runs rampant through American and Canadian cities, much to the delight of Arab extremists who hail it as evidence of Allah's Providence and Will.

A sea accident involving a People's Republic of China submarine and a United States aircraft carrier creates more tension between the two superpowers, bringing ever closer the threat of thermal nuclear war!

A bold new group of North American terrorists pull off attacks on nearly every major nuclear power plant around the globe, on or about next New Year's Eve.

European air prices drop dramatically due to terrorist threats, creating panic in North American companies and thus making stock in Euro lines plunge! (No pun intended.)

Medieval punishments such as beheading, hanging and "drawing and quartering" become popular again! For the torture, rape and mutilation of children and animals it is appropriate, and then after that something truly gruesome should be done to them!

I see a tall, light-gray brick office building – not unlike the Empire State or the Chrysler buildings – but not necessarily so, toppling to the ground...don't know whether New York? Chicago? Toronto?... May be an earthquake, maybe terrorists. (Have I covered everything?) Great loss of life and property. (I think New York and Toronto!)

A great suspension bridge that lights up at night collapses and falls. The cause *will not* be natural!

A high ranking Communist general is assassinated, bringing us ever closer to the brink!

Mickey Mouse and **Donald Duck** become more famous in 2006 than ever they were in the past, doing the talk-show circuit — and, unbelievably, meeting the U.S. President! (...Come to think of it, not so *unbelievable* after all, as one cartoon character to another.)

We are nanoseconds away from discovering *the-e-e* Universal formula fuel that will make anything we now use for power, obsolete. This fuel shall be as advanced as comparing a calculator to an abacus.

I have always predicted that the compound number "11-11" holds the key to Eternity, Man's survival on Earth or any where else in the Cosmos. This *is* Heaven's answer. And now possibly the "String-Theory," an as yet unconfirmed "*11*"-*dimensional* model of the Universe (and Universi) – also referred to as *the theory of everything,* may – nay, *does* hold that key which will unlock the Pearly Gates of Heaven...so to speak.

News headlines world-wide soon scream:– "Proof-positive is coming that the late **Princess Diana** was indeed pregnant with equally late **Dodi al Fayed**'s baby when they died a fiery vehicular death in France!" Weeks prior to her tragic death, former GLOBE editor **Joe Mullins** and GLOBE reporter **Ken Harrell** asked *yours truly* what the future held for the happy couple. I said: "Not so happy.... I see a *fatal*, fiery vehicular accident!, a series of postage stamps with her face on them (which were issued following her death) and, most importantly, I sense she is pregnant – a girl!" This conversation was duly recorded by the above mentioned GLOBE staff members.

The last Pope will admit women to the priesthood.

Cuckoldry becomes ever more acceptable as dynamic women take on roles once reserved for "men." Men will sit by passively and accept this fate-worse-than-death from their wives and partners, who'll flaunt their affairs in their faces. As someone once said: "Women *pretend* to be what men *really are!*" (emotional wimps!), until the next world war, when they'll once again reverse roles and run to hide behind their skirts and their men!

Credit and debit card fraud increases exponentially over the next few years to the point where a new system is introduced worldwide. This probably refers to the biblical numbers 666 and 999 (or was it 888?) mentioned in the Christian Bible's book of Revelation, by St. John, the Divine.

As today's religions eventually go the way of the dinosaurs, our literature becomes revered as priceless art in much the same way rare documents are regarded today. The *new* religion is to begin with the return of the Star-Travelers.

A fiery asteroid strikes Earth on flatlands near the foot of mountains surrounded by desert. An eerie aquamarine light issues forth.

With the rise of global temperature, squalls and tornados are permanent threats to crops. This unpredictable weather is *such* that *Bio-farming* becomes the way of the future.

Tidal waves, as seen only in movies, become reality! Monstrous circles of water engulf populated cities as Earth's polarities shift. Los Angeles swallowed up in one great gulp of an earthquake! Nevada, Arizona, become new coastlines. (But then again, could be just a "scene" from yet another disaster movie....) Or not!

Yet another underground transit system is suddenly stricken!... People sick and dying! This catastrophe can be compared to 9 /11!... Terrorist group responsible to be flushed out and killed in violent fire-fight! (Are there any other kind?)

A strange insect appears on the horizon from never ending

excavation projects. The world's most brilliant scientists are puzzled! Although not fatal to humans, this bug – the size of a hummingbird – thrives on other insects (locusts etc.) that destroy crops, thereby aiding farmers and mankind in general.

Food becomes a huge entertainment draw! –Los Angeles, Las Vegas, Toronto and New York. People *yearn* for the warm security of the comfort foods they once knew and loved as children.

Euthanasia centers for the physically, mentally and hopelessly ugly will spring up worldwide.

Due to global warming, the Arctic Circle becomes more temperate thereby attracting peoples of the world to it in a grand Exodus, as big city air quality turns deadly! (Not to mention any names – Los Angeles!)

Before his trial, **Saddam Hussein's** enemies smuggle weapons through Palestine to use against the former Iraqi dictator, in an attempt to send him quickly to Paradise – or to the "other place" – in a blaze of glory. It fails.... Still, a woman may bring about his demise.

America will attack Iran about January or February, 2006.

British Prime Minister **Tony Blair's** son, **Nicky,** succeeds very well in show business — but startling news about his "personal" life will surprise the world, even his father (to say the least).

Tragic circumstances prevent **Prince Charles** and his legitimate progeny (**Willy** and **Harry**) from ascending the British throne. **Prince Andrew** shall reign supreme! Yet news surfaces that "Charlie" has a teenage love child whom the whole world will come to know.

Leftist rebels in Columbia attempt to assassinate U.S. President Bush for his support of the Colombian government, but then realize they need only wait until he not only shoots himself in the foot, but in both feet - and the head as well!

A blackout hits North America - again, wiping out the continent's entire power supply. Martial law is declared as military forces are called in to halt rioting and looting. However, nine months later the population increases ten-fold!

Nuclear explosions in South Korea put surrounding

countries at risk from fallout. *Beware this country!*

Saudi Arabia suddenly turns from America. Soldiers stationed there are taken prisoner and publicly tortured. This brings us to... Ta-dah! – Armageddon!!!

America will completely militarize Israel and defend her against all on-comers.

Neo-Nazi and right-wing extremists stage biggest rally ever, at Stuttgart.

Germany declares a Fourth Reich... elects a man who much resembles "the Fuhrer," for nostalgic reasons. (...How touching!)

Like a great yellow tidal wave the mighty red juggernaut stirs.... World – watch out!

Aids continues to spread across Africa, killing tens of thousands until it burns out, as did the black plague of Europe and London (1666).

Fidel Castro falls gravely ill from a poisoning attempt — yet recovers! This is followed by an unexpected reconciliation with America.

Leftist-rebel **Michael Moore** in grave danger of succumbing to a fatal disease which appears quite natural.

Over the sea, with tremendous speed, comes a man who's gold and holy, yet to the believers, this great deceiver, will break the hearts of many. (Another wannabe anti-Christ!)

A meteor from deep space enters Earth's atmosphere over Las Vegas, Nevada, with the crack of a thousand thunders and lights up the town brighter than all of its neon combined! The giant space rock – composed of unidentifiable properties – rains down on the desert turning the arid land into a lush oasis.

Documents time-sealed in the vaults of the CIA will be released to the public and shock the world when it's discovered that not only did **Bush Sr.** (then head of the C.I.A.) know beforehand about the intended assassination of **John F. Kennedy,** but was complicit in it by not taking action to prevent the disaster!

Osama bin Laden's hiding place discovered! His features were altered under orders from very, *very* prominent members of the U.S. government and others residing in "The Land of the Free" who were in on the 9 / 11 attacks. All the 9/11 conspiracy predictions will soon come to light. Names of those involved will *shock* Americans and Canadians!

A second moon appears in the heavens of such unbelievable size it produces tidal waves that turn once land-locked nations into islands!

Men will fight each other, then unite and battle the Evil One, Who is in turn destroyed by the Son!

Space aliens will abduct astrophysicists and replace them with their own in order to prevent Earthlings from successfully making intergalactic journeys!

Great Mother Russia rises from its ashes like the mythical Phoenix, continuing in its age-old quest of waging war against its neighbors – the rest of the world!

The Israeli wall effectively results in dividing the world as the new Iron Curtain, plunging us back to the darkness of another cold war.

On the Jordan River a boatload of Jewish children strikes a submerged object and explodes! Everyone thinks it an act of terrorism! Discovered too late, this act of Fate, lets loose the Dogs of War!

In America, a giant concrete dam bursts! Great flood waters throughout the arid land! (Hoover Dam? Boulder Dam?)

Mount Rushmore (heads of the four U.S. Presidents in South Dakota) will be severely damaged by saboteurs.

Interminably long, frustrating waits on freeways caused by vehicular accidents in which no one can move until tow trucks arrive to remove the mess, will become a thing of the past with the implementation of jet-propelled helicopter "tow-trucks" that simply airlift the cars, trucks, boats (boats?) planes or trains – off the freeway.

MEDICINE/SCIENCE

There's a potential killer in town – PROZAC! And it may not particularly respect children. Because of suspicion surrounding the alleged link between high incidences of suicide and this strong "antidepressant," I predict this controversial drug will be permanently removed from the pharmaceutical cornucopia.

Pretty, blue-eyed Allison Millar of Toronto, Canada, was put on Prozac by her psychiatrist. She was 14-years old, and at 14 she died, by hanging herself, alongside her favorite teddy bear. Prozac certainly did not help her, and may have contributed to her death. Allison Millar, my cousin.

It will be discovered that many "altered mental states" (including schizophrenia) are the result of *finely-tuned, ultra-sensitive* Electrical impulses interacting "badly" with Electrical particles and waves of other people, which are then carried to and fro through the Ether – the Ether which is *also* Electrically charged and is both a transmitter and receiver.

Treatment and control will be a mild alternating current, much like a pacemaker, that'll be triggered by any unusual or aberrant power spike anywhere in the brain, rendering the patient reasonable and content. In short, it's the return of 1930's Electric Shock Therapy – sneaking in through the back door!

Severed or amputated limbs will grow back, even on people born without them, through the re-discovery of the amphibian gene.

Schizophrenia all but eradicated! ESP becomes the new science, sans religion and superstition, and is placed in the realm of physics, where it belongs!

Artificial sweeteners used in colas and other beverages are removed from the marketplace because of their link to cancer. And cell phones the world over will be modified for the same reason, the carcinoma threat caused by deadly radiation emission over *long periods* of time. This baby-boomer generation won't be around long enough to warrant any worry, but youngsters who keep the phone to their ear for hours on end are most certainly in danger! My advice is, "SAY WHAT YOU MUST AS BRIEFLY AS POSSIBLE, HANG UP, AND YOU'LL BE FINE." If you need to talk at length, use a landline.

Discovery of a unifying, supra anti-rejection drug that perfectly imitates human tissue structure and spreads evenly throughout the body's cellular fabric, will enable all organ transplants to take perfectly even on the first attempt, regardless of donor source. Cloning embryos for organ harvesting is the next logical step and will become reality, once superstitious and archaic religious notions are put aside.

A horrible error in science debunks the psychotropic medication trend. More people suddenly experience fatal effects. Lawsuits deluge governments as people finally fight back! This marks the beginning of the end of prozac-like "anti-depressant" drugs and the pseudo-science of psychiatry and psychoanalysis, in general.

Discovery of a new antibiotic greatly changes the complexion of medicine. For cancer and Alzheimer patients – new hope! This is a giant step towards the total eradication of many deadly diseases.

Star-traveling Gods resurrect dead cells through methods of DNA engineering, activating life's essence from the bones of the living and the dead!

A solution (sodium in nature) is discovered that sticks to plaque-like substance which causes Alzheimer's. It stops a moment to photograph it (the substance) then leaves before causing damage to the patient.

For the past forty-some odd years I have happily, accurately and most persistently predicted major medical breakthroughs in the areas of glaucoma, spinal cord injuries and, indeed, most of the "electrically interrupted" neurological diseases such as Multiple Sclerosis, Muscular Dystrophy, Adreno-Leuko Dystrophy and, most popular of all, Amiotrophic Lateral Sclerosis (Lou Gehrigs's disease). Although progress is slow, I am convinced that we are on the very threshold of a major cure-all for these terrible scourges. So once again I utter my own favorite slogan, "Dead legs *will walk again!*"

Hardening of the arteries (angiopathic ischemia), a disease of the elderly in which the walls of the veins and arteries become rigid, will be eradicated by the injection of a miraculous new drug which lubricates and re-elasticizes the arterial system. The elderly will enjoy all the activities they did when they were 30 – even rigorous sex!

Believe it or not – men will give birth!

From the Cosmos an Electrical cure-all for the litany of

human diseases – including MS (Multiple Sclerosis, MD (Muscular Dystrophy) and ALS (Lou Gehrigs's Disease) – "and death shall be no more."

A dynamic breakthrough in the treatment – and cure – of dreaded leukemia! A single common cause for the various types is discovered, and then a "single-thread" injection solves the problem.

World-wide cessation of rain forest destruction! The sudden realization of the magnitude of the ozone layer destruction and plethora of possible new cures for the multifarious diseases that plague mankind will stop the practice of clear-cutting these jungles of priceless value!

Doctors who discovered the AIDS cocktail (including Dr. David Ho) will stumble on to a more potent form of this vaccine that'll halt the disease in its tracks for good!

Hectic living and the looming threat of terrorist attacks has everyone seeking new remedies to keep up with life's pressures. A more philosophical attitude about life and death will prevail and give Westerners courage to carry on and fight back!

Alarming news about the plastic surgery industry! Weak-minded people who seek *unnecessary* surgery. Countless people die on operating tables! Surgeons fined for performing dangerous procedures without explaining risks – all for money! Complete physical makeovers become pandemic!!

Teen drug-use escalates in a futile attempt to escape life's realities. Slow down; take a "reality" check. Life *is* tough! Learn to deal with it!

Global warming takes tragic tolls as air thickens into soupy sludge! People wander the globe, zombie-like, in search of clean, sweet air. Wealthy people purchase large tracts of land in the far North – Alaska, Northwest Territories – to this end. The poor remain on Earth as it becomes a dying planet. *New life flourishes in* our own solar system... "...and the *meek* [which rhymes with *weak*] shall inherit the Earth." (Christian Bible: Revelations)

A Mighty Mouse U-25 super nutrition pill is invented to offset nourishment-loss from conventional sources. (As a kid watching "Mighty Mouse" cartoons at the movies, I always wondered what was in that little pill box he wore on his belt buckle that transformed him from a weak little mouse on crutches, into the "Hulk" of super mice. Now I think I know: it must have been a combination of "Speed and Steroids!")

With delusional and idealistic Neptune transiting Aquarius, left wing Shangri-la "love and let love" views will generate a sense of "well-being" over the next seven years, to offset the negativity of the Baby-Boomer generation created by Uranus going through Pisces. "Love" communes, much like those of the 60s, will spring up World-wide.

A new spread of Creutzfeldt-Jakob disease (Mad Cow Disease) develops a natural immunity to *itself*, from which medical science will in turn create a vaccine.

ENTERTAINMENT

Celebrity deaths: **Dick Clark**, **Mohammad Ali**, docu-king **Michael Moore**, former presidents **Jimmy Carter** and **Gerald Ford**; ditto former British Prime Minister "Iron Lady" **Margaret Thatcher**, jazz piano great **Oscar Peterson**, thespians **Sidney Poitier** and **Lauren Bacall**, **Woody Allan** (suspicious death, his wife is suspect!)

Kevin Spacey will either come all the way out of the closet or jump right back in – but too late! Soon all the world will know the expression "as gay as a goose"—or geese, if one is promiscuous. In fact, he may actually *keep* a goose as a pet!

Kate Hudson will announce she is a born again Jehovah's Witness and proceeds from house to house preaching to the "fed up." Although she once considered a nose-job, this will no longer be necessary as a result of natural attrition from doors slamming in her face!

Liam Neeson ("Schindler's List") is in danger of being swept away by a tsunami more humongous even than the one which struck Sri-Lanka! Yet he'll live to talk about it.

Pearl Harbor star hunk **Ben Affleck** to be afflicted with an undiagnosable itch that leaves doctors baffled. It is so severe that a strait jacket is required to prevent him from tearing off his skin, covered in a pimply, red rash that disappears as quickly as it appeared! Go figure.

Ben E. King – legendary rhythm & blues singer and composer of the now perennial favorite "Stand by Me," will be honored with a Lifetime Achievement Award for his musical contributions to the very fabric of our culture. I see a medallion on long, colored ribbon, worn around his neck.

Jacqueline Stallone, famed astrologer and mother of superstar actor **Sylvester Stallone**, makes international headlines in 2006 when she becomes the darling of European aristocracy through her accurate planetary prognostications. I also see a highly successful television show, beamed around the world. She'll also become a mother again! (Through adoption, that is.... Although, stranger things have happened.)

Sylvester Stallone must guard his health. *Moderation* is the key word. He'll need to conserve energy because I see him moving ahead by "leaps and bounds" – literally! New Rambo and Rocky flicks are in his future! *(predicted last June in 2004 edition of STARGAZER)

Director **Norman** "what's-he-done-lately" **Jewison** to be hospitalized with serious respiratory problems brought on by heart failure,that a heart-pacer corrects.

Rompin' **Ronnie Hawkins** survives yet another year with his inoperable pancreatic cancer. He never ceases to amaze!

Courtney Cox finally wins eating fetish battle by having her lips stitched shut for six months! (Don't laugh – it'll work!) If she doesn't, her twisted love for food will exceed her desire to be thin and thus destroy her career.

Beloved evangelist crusader **Billy Graham** will enter God's Kingdom in 2006... (probably against his will).

Last year I predicted "**Oprah Winfrey** to be awarded the Nobel Prize or a Lifetime Achievement award from the Kennedy Centre for the Performing Arts." Her name has since been put up for the Nobel Honor and I stand by my prophecy. Oprah may be happy but she's certainly not "gay."

Pop princess **Britney Spears** to end up broke and on welfare in short order as her husband **Kevin Federline**, flies the coop! Her situation can be likened to Whitney Houston's and her "better half," **Bobby Brown** – both husbands frustrated wannabes. Spears will sue for divorce and eventually marry a peer of the realm.

Bill Baldwin gets punched out at a shopping plaza after verbally abusing a young woman who bangs into his shopping cart. Unknown to him her lover, a serious female bodybuilder on steroids, taps him on the shoulder and cold cocks him!

Eric Alexandre Stephane, the love child of Monaco's Playboy Prince **Albert** and **Nicole Coste,** is in grave danger! "Purist" supporters of the Grimaldi dynasty are plotting against mother and child – even as I speak! There is fear the Togo born beauty and her son will not much longer see the light of day... Indeed, murder *most foul...* to look accidental!!

I see a terrible helicopter mishap around diva **Celine Dion.** Although not injured, she is merely shaken (not stirred), the near death experience will change her attitude about life and death, free-will or none – and all that stuff. Plus it will certainly change her ideas about travel – trains, boats but definitely not planes!

Rolling Stones' founding father **Keith Richards** develops potentially fatal blood disorder!

"Chocolate Factory" man **Johnny Depp** to grieve over **Keith Richards** who was to play father figure in "Pirates of the Caribbean" sequel. However, this grief is merely a dress rehearsal for what's to come – grief exacerbated by the drowning death of a young boy!

Pop star **Justin Timberlake** segues from "Pop to Stock" (broker) in 2006 – discovering his true talent lies in big business – "wheeling and dealing." A gorgeous blond, wife-to-be, is also in his future.

The King's daughter, **Lisa Marie Presley**, will never make it vocally (sounds too much like Greta Garbo) but will as a dare-devil, Evel Knievel-type racing fiend – cars, motorcycles, etc. She'll also suffer the requisite number of broken bones. First injuries will hit the news in a matter of weeks!

Dan Akroyd seeks serious roles as he ages. Although Hollywood hasn't quite forgotten him, it'll be a rather slow climb up the other side of the ladder of success to the pinnacle of stardom he once enjoyed, since he's now pickier about scripts. Ultimately he will arrive, through historical (not hysterical) roles.

A hardcore right wing women's group attempts to "out" chanteuse **Anne Murray**, the barefoot contessa.

Robin Williams experiences a *cancer* scare but then breaths a sigh of relief when it's discovered his x-rays were "accidentally" switched with those of a terminal patient. If this snafu isn't enough to kill him – then surely the shock to his heart might!

Brad Pitt's former squeeze, **Jennifer Aniston**, is beset by a stalker! This character is extremely dangerous and every precaution should be taken to protect her until he is caught! The monster hails from Great Britain.

Beverly Hills 90210 star **Jason Priestly** serves jail time after a drug or drink induced fatal accident. A young man is killed!

David Clayton-Thomas, of "Blood, Sweat & Tears" fame, to complete autobiography and TV documentary which brings him new found fame. It's a movie-made-for-TV about his life. This newfound stardom forces him to reorganize the band for yet another world tour!

Nancy Sinatra, darling daughter of "old smoothie" **Frank**, will make a steady comeback up the corporate showbiz ladder with a new video and fabulous nostalgic Las Vegas show featuring songs by her infamous dad, on film, as he sings side-by-side – *"live"* – with Nancy. Older folk eat it up! I see big, BIG success all around her!

Aviator star **Leonardo Di Caprio** learns a few lessons in humility when the father of a little girl, who wanted his autograph, knocks him on his keester for demanding payment from the disappointed child.

Billy Bob Thorton's spectacular talents will be recognized and rewarded at the 2006 Academy Awards. It'll be universal karmic payback for being robbed of the erstwhile Best Actor Oscar for "Swing Blade," which he so richly deserved.

Shirley MacLaine, "other-worldly" star of Bewitched and alleged necromancer (communicator of the dead), will star – along with brother **Warren Beatty** – in one more movie with religious and spiritual overtones before she herself ascends that heavenly plateau.

Al Pacino, perennial "Godfather" favorite, will star in yet another sequel to the previous three incarnations of moviedom's most powerful crime family, the Corleones. Even though in GFIII it appeared that "Michael" died outdoors while sitting in his favorite chair before flopping on to the ground like a dead mackerel, wonder of wonders, he's not really dead at all! – but very much alive and only in a diabetic coma! After this film wraps, Mr. Pacino will undergo deep psychotherapy – suffering a very serious identity crisis!

News that French-Canadian Chanteuse **Celine Dion** "is expecting" will be forthcoming early in the year. But good news is often off-set by bad. Unfortunately her manager/husband, **Rene Angelil**, will once again be stricken by deadly cancer – melanoma! For two years it'll be touch and go, he passes, she marries again to bear yet more children – twins!

Keanu Reeves assays one last time his dream of becoming a singer. He fails miserably! But his debut on Broadway gets rave reviews!

Actor **Donald Sutherland** has serious eye problems, specifically tumors!

Coming on the heels of screenwriter **Joe** ("Show Girls") **Eszterhas's** repentance, Hollywood will place a ban on smoking in movies. The move to be applauded by bleeding heart liberals and attacked by civil liberties unions. (So what else is new?)

Sir Elton John is threatened with the loss of his *knight*hood due to "nasty *nights* in the hood" rumours. (His neighbourhood, of course.) But all is forgiven by the (other) Queen, everything being a huge "misunderstanding." (Ny-uck, ny-uck – sure it is!)

Alison Carey, Pop diva **Mariah Carey**'s pill poppin' sister, will never overcome her drug and booze addictions – eventually succumbing to them and, of course, breaking her family's heart. There's no hope for a woman completely devoid of maternal instinct. (Her two children have been legally adopted by Mariah and their mom, Pat.) When its "finished," Mariah Carey will contribute time and money to organizations specializing in drug recovery programs, in an attempt to compensate for the loss of her sister by trying to save lost souls.

Julia Roberts loses several family members simultaneously. (I "see" fire... I see her standing beside two graves.) She is inconsolable! Let's hope it's just another movie.

Proof-positive is forthcoming that **Terri Schiavo**, the comatose woman allowed by her husband to slowly die of starvation on television for all the world to see, was indeed murdered by her "better" half.

"Great White Hope" star **James Earl Jones**, who portrayed Jack Johnson, possibly the greatest fighter who ever lived, will hang up his gloves for good so he can enter those pearly gates unencumbered.

Mia Farrow, Woody Allen's erstwhile squeeze, need never worry about her polio reoccurring, that dreaded disease she suffered as a child. Indeed, she'll actually grow stronger as the years pass (unlike the rest of us). Watch for Ms. Farrow to hit the world stage in a successful global television appeal to "Save the Children", which proves to be even more successful than funnyman Jerry Lewis' nationally televised money drive for "Jerry's Kids with Multiple Sclerosis". Mia's show truly will be international in every sense.

Comedian/director **Woody Allen** requires throat surgery! Perhaps cancer or perhaps once again he cuts his own throat through scandal! (Like a lamb carrying a knife to the slaughter!)

Something *snaps* **Martha Stewart** as she slowly develops acute paranoid schizophrenia because of negative publicity. She'll spend three months in mental rehab.

Movies and television move toward scripts with positive themes that'll have a good influence on the weak-minded who identify too much with characters in film. Then the public cannot blame Hollywood dream-makers for violent acts committed by morons.

Because of over-saturation, only superstars will emerge successfully from the new avenue of Reality TV.

Tom Cruise's career takes off like a rocket – literally! – when he signs on for a space shuttle ride, insisting (as I do) that God was and is a Star-Traveler whom he wants to meet face to face. (Old Tom is a SCIENTOLOGIST, after all, as is John Travolta.)

Teen sensation **Hillary Duff** continues to take the world by storm – outdoing even **Lindsey Lohan** and **Britney Spears** but, like many young celebrities who acquire too much too soon, she'll slowly slide into the dark, seedy underworld of drugs, booze and "gangstas," finding the element therein infinitely more interesting and exciting than mere showbiz.

Septuagenarian **Regis Philbin** keels over dead of a heart attack (or stroke), on camera during a taping of his show – "Live! With Regis and Kelly." Ratings will be *high* as people are glued to their TVs waiting for an encore – that is, until they realize it's a one-time performance only. No encore. Unless they decide to rename the show: "Live! with Kelly, Dead! with Regis" ...Anything for a buck.

Dick van Dyke show alumnae **Mary Tyler Moore**'s health vastly improves with the surgical implantation of an artificial pancreas-like device that halts her diabetes in its tracks! The treatment makes world headlines and puts her in position to host the first in a series of globally televised health shows!

Angelina Jolie's dream house in the South of France – near Cannes, site of the annual world film festival – will be destroyed by a cataclysmic earthquake! Luckily she and hubby **Brad Pitt** will not be home when disaster comes calling.... Not so lucky, though, are the thousands of natives and visitors.

Tom Cruise and **Katie Holmes** suddenly split and again begin the rumours of his sexual persuasion and peccadilloes.

Basic Instinct's **Sharon Stone** loses much of her allure when Basic Instinct II hits theatres. Long since past the age of that "je ne sais quoi," she'll become a national laughing stock. Sharon! let the illusion remain. "If it ain't broken, don't fix it!"

The "Wheel of (mis)Fortune" continues to spin backwards for **Vanna White** as yet another marital disaster awaits her. After surviving a series of bad love affairs – including the violent deaths of at least two of them – she's gonna have her heart *shocked* and broken when she discovers her fiancé/husband **Michael Kaye** has an entirely *different* lifestyle, unbeknownst to Vanna. By the way, I don't believe Michael Kaye is related to the late, great, movie comic **Danny Kaye** who was, incidentally – gay! (Hmmm... was "Kay

Gay?" ...seems to flow!) Get a dog next time, Vanna, get a dog... much better company.

Michael Moore, director of the documentary "Fahrenheit 9/11," which is highly critical of President Bush's Sept.11 actions (or non-actions), is in imminent physical danger! Michaels's best insurance against death is to broadcast to the world that "Should anything happen to me – even if I'm struck by lightning in bed! – it'll be Bush's doing."

Box-office boxing bomb, **Cinderella Man**, about former world heavyweight boxing champion James J. Braddock (a Canadian, eh!), and starring **Russell Crowe**, will eventually become a cult favorite, such as **Casablanca**, **King Kong** – et al.

The Beastie Boys' (Mike D.,MCA, Adrock) views on Tibetan Freedom will change drastically when they are injured on a good-will trip to Tibet by guerilla fighters.

Busty "Baywatch" babe **Pamela Anderson's** rekindled relationship with ex-husband, drummer **Tommy Lee**, will end tragically! A murder-suicide, not unlike the late Sid Vicious of the punk rock band "The Sex Pistols" and his wife. Now *there* was a match made in hell!

Diminutive **Danny DeVito** becomes taller after a stunning breakthrough in orthopedic surgery that allows bone grafts to be inserted between knees and ankles, creating six more inches of height. Anti-rejection drugs are not necessary since the grafts are taken from his own femurs!

Booty-shakin' diva **Beyoncé** will devote much time and talent to children's orphanages world-wide. She definitely has a soft spot for kids and, like super-moms Josephine Baker and Mia Farrow, eventually will adopt a Baker's dozen or so.

Kirstie Alley, because of her ability to quickly gain "bulk" like Olympic power lifters, takes up bodybuilding (sans steroids) in an all out effort to not only trim down but tone up her muscles as well. The result will be astonishing! She'll enter – and win – a local female bodybuilding pageant and then go on to open a string of gyms across America that will bear her name, maybe something like: "Gird Your Loins with Kristie! (Some people never "loin?" – That's bad, so bad.)

Crotch-grabbin' **Roseanne Barr** will gain so much weight that she'll be able to sit on her *own* lap! So much weight that if she attempts suicide by shooting herself in the heart under the left breast, she'll probably blow her kneecap off!

Watch for the return of "Lil Abner" comics and a blockbuster movie featuring all the beloved characters: Lil Abner, Daisy Mae, Marryin' Sam and – last but not least – Sadie Hawkins, named for the infamous dance in her name and dedicated to loser women the world over.

Matt Damon lends his name to a string of fruit juice bars across America. Very successful!

Mike Myers lends his initials to M&Ms and becomes pitchman for the colorful little candies.

Shania Twain, Canada's songbird of the North, knocks the pins out from under beloved snowbird of yesteryear **Anne Murray**, when the Timmins, Ontario native superstar achieves even greater status in the coming years.

Lacrosse is the next trend for the young Hollywood in Crowd, leaving poker in second place. However, due to their lack of experience there is no end to broken bones which they'll proudly display as a rite of passage.

"The Island" star **Scarlett Johansson** is held hostage while visiting a *real* tropical island with her real-life boyfriend. While trying to enjoy some down time, an unexpected political coup takes place and she is grabbed and taken! Local Troops eventually rescue the lovely lass but unfortunately not in time to save the boyfriend... (But again, it may be just a *scene* from a future celluloid adventure!)

Kevin Costner wins Oscar in a brand new category called "The Year's Most Boring Actor!"

Ricardo Montalban to pass in 2006 after he falls from his wheelchair... while hand gliding!

A stunning (quite believable) proposition that **Elvis Presley** is not dead and buried in the grave at Graceland – but alive and well! Someone may have cloned Elvis, using DNA from tissue obtained during his post mortem, or he himself fathered another child years ago so that the offspring, now in his late 20s or early 30s, is uncannily like the "father." The world will be buzzin'!!

Corpulent country singer **Wynonna Judd** finally trims down to her former slender self after a cardiac scare that's commensurate with her cud-chewing! This puts the fear of God in her – and *her* on a permanent exercise regime.

Late movie and television cowboy and cowgirl stars **Roy Rogers** and wife **Dale Evans** (– that's "late" as in dead, not "late" as in late-night old movies on TV –) are pushing up polyurethane – artificial turf – instead of real grass in their final resting place at Sunset Hills Memorial Park, Apple Valley, California. (– I just love these euphemisms for being dead and buried!) Chills run up and down the spines of the cemetery owners when their phony grass turns brown, wilts and actually dies! It's the legendary Hollywood couple demonstrating their disapproval until the real stuff is once again "laid down." (...Br-r-r-r!)

"Anchorman" **Will Farrell**, an alumnus of Saturday Night Live, will be offered the role that sends his career through the stratosphere and makes him the highest paid male actor in Hollywood. That role will be **Stan Laurel**, one half of the greatest slapstick comedy team of all time, Laurel and Hardy (or who we, as kids, used to call: "Fat and Skinny").

Tatum O'Neal, former child star and daughter of tough guy actor **Ryan O'Neal**, will be reborn as a serious Broadway actress in a hit play that will run for years. When she was a child I read her palms – along with those of the late RICHARD BURTON (they were starring in "Circle of Two") – and commented that she would endure a stormy marriage (was married to and divorced from tennis bad boy **John McEnroe**), then develop but overcome a serious drug problem (which she did and has) and after a lengthy hiatus between acting jobs (which lasted years!), go on to a spectacular career – far greater than that which she enjoyed as a child and which is now just about to launch! I remember we had a discussion about the pronunciation of the word *cherub* and thought her, even then, a talented and extremely precocious child.

Karate -chopping **Chuck Norris** runs into problems with the IRS who'll be more than happy to *hack* a few million dollars from his accounts for (allegedly) non-payment of taxes. Although the "Walker: Texas Ranger" star may *kick* and *scream,* his bankroll will be considerably diminished. Cheer up, Chucky baby, you can always *knockout* a few more movies – which I predict you shall.

Calypso singing legend and "Porgy and Bess" star **Harry Belafonte** will be led into the best possible aspects of world politics. (Politics with "good aspects"?!) He will meet with world figures and be hailed as a peacekeeper before leaving this old world behind. (When else? – *after* he leaves this old world behind?) Kudos and awards shall be heaped upon him, and all the world shall revere him.

"Cinderella Man" **Russell Crowe,** for all his hot-headedness will surprise the world with generous donations of money to the less fortunate, the poor and the indigent. A well-known foundation will award him for his humanitarian ways and shall set one up in his name.

Due to her ongoing battle with diabetes, "Gothika" and "The Dorothy Dandrige Story" star, **Halle Barry,** will suffer debilitating eye problems requiring emergency surgery to save her sight! Despite health setbacks, her career will continue to blossom as she grows into the grande dame of theatre.

Cher will find herself enmeshed in a terrible tragedy involving her gay daughter.

Robert Downey, Jr. is currently enjoying some success in the comedy movie: "Bang Bang, Kiss Kiss," but he has wasted so much time rehabilitating himself that the movie industry is moving on without him. Even though his personal antics were at least as entertaining as his movies, the bad boy of Hollywood will temporarily slip into obscurity, as did **David Caruso** and **John Travolta** (or "Revolta," as some prefer). His only hope is that he'll be rescued from oblivion by a television series. And so he shall!

The turbulent life and times of actress/singer **Eartha "Catwoman" Kitt** will be acknowledged with a special lifetime achievement award that *cat*-apults her back into world prominence! Your career is about to start up again, my dear, and that's pur-r-r-ty good.

Sean Connery to be invested with the title "honorary fellow" by Edinburgh University, and a chair and scholarship dedicated in his name as a native son of Scotland.

After all the tragedies (multiple sclerosis, car accidents) that have befallen **Annette Funicello**, Mickey Mouse Club alumnae and star of numerous 1960s Beach Party movies, I am certain (– hopeful –) she will yet make a full recovery as a result of marvelous new treatments coming down the pike that shall halt the destruction of the insulatory myelin which surrounds and protects each nerve ending, and may perhaps even reverse the disease's damage!

Daredevil **Evel Knievel** is so darn tough that he'll undergo – and survive – a double lung transplant then return to his (un-)usual lifestyle of *risking his life* for a living.

John Travolta's still in danger flying that private jet! A hard landing is due him – and I don't mean figuratively – if he keeps flying at night!

Harrison Ford is a terrific actor and a wonderful human being. But alas, I sense an injury to him or to one of his sons, around horses. I would admonish him to take great care over the next few months if he chooses to horseback ride, whether in real life or while filming scenes around horses. Also warn his sons. We don't want another **Christopher Reeve** tragedy.

Former "Cheers" star **Kelsey Grammar** also has had so many family tragedies that it's a wonder he's still sane! A berserk gunman killed his dad; three teens robbed, raped then stabbed to death his sister; and his two brothers were eaten by sharks! (And I don't mean lawyers!) Gradually he will segue toward the world of spirit, becoming himself an excellent channeller to the other side, which in turn brings him peace of mind.

Mythic actress **Shelly Winters** to be hailed a living legend while *indeed still living!* Many parties in her honor. She'll be feted to death!

Acquitted wife killer **O.J. Simpson** is found dead! Incredibly, rumors will abound that his children, **Sydney** and **Justin**, are responsible! But in time, information leaks that the "mob hit" him for unpaid gambling debts exceeding millions! The Juice's death will be an incentive for other like-minded investors to pay their debts promptly.

Star Trek's late **James** ("Beam me up, Scotty") **Doohan's** fame begins to take on mythic proportions now that he has ascended the heavenly latitudes. I see "Scotty angels," "Scotty Dolls" and even "Scotty G.I. Joes" – depicting his heroic efforts on D-Day, June 6, 1943 on Juno Beach, where he was shot seven times – and survived!

The world soon learns of **Jude Law's** not so charming....side when he gets into an altercation with police who (– wait for it! –) charge him with ..."improper use of a public facility" in one of the stalls of the "Men's" room! (Hmmm.)

Unfortunately I see booze, pills, suicide attempts, drugs and death *around* **Melanie Griffith**, mostly triggered by the death of a child. (Again, hopefully just a scene from an upcoming movie.)

"Die Hard" star **Bruce Willis** will leave us in the very same manner another legendary cinematic celebrity from that Great Golden Hollywood Era left us, **Errol Flynn**, who died in the throes aboard his yacht – and aboard his seventeen-year-old girlfriend in Vancouver Harbor, British Columbia, Canada. He was 50, at the time! The medical examiner said he had the "insides" of an eighty-year-old. But what a way to go! If I were granted a choice between dying from a speeding train or going the way old Errol went, YOU JUST GOTTA KNOW WHICH LINE UP I'M GONNA BE IN!!! (Amen)

Because of the terrorist attacks in London, British television becomes the new thing to watch as young people and elite groups surge forth as the next British invasion. Remember the Beatles? The new English Superstars will emerge from shows centering around rescues and rescuers – police, fire departments, citizens – in the aftermath of the Underground explosions, and shows that proceed there from.

Hollywood stars to flex muscles... brains, not buttocks! **Jodie Foster** has a Harvard degree, **James Woods** and **Gena Davis** are both Mensa members — to mention a few! The coming trend of Hollywood success will be determined by intelligence, leaving dum-dums with nice bum-bums, out in the cold.

Jack Nicholson faces very serious heart problems, including bypass surgery..

Michael Jackson accidentally finds himself in the eye of a terrible fire-fight while trying to drum up new business in the Middle East. And for a while this lends him some cachet.

Jennifer Lopez (J. Lo) will suffer devastating effects of liposuction, used on her butt to reduce excess baggage and smooth out wrinkly tissue caused by cellulite deposits... a sort of facelift in reverse. But – and no *bum* intended — a serious staff infection from instruments not properly autoclaved (sterilized) leaves her best ass-et the size of an elephant's, blown way out of proportion. Bummer!

Madonna to enter politics and surprises the world by being good at it! Tough, but fair; so "don't cry for me, Argentina!" (or Britain or America or wherever.)

Raging Bull superstar **Robert DeNiro** to star in new flick called "The Sobfather," a spoof about gay gangsters in New York – but focusing on the head fag of five families, the capo di tutti i capi. This'll be a hard-hitting, fast-paced movie in which the action rapidly oscillates between the combatants as they slap beat and shoot each other with plastic bats and paint guns, and in the end – all die of heartbreak for slapping each other!

Philip Seymour Hoffman will do for "Capote" (author of best selling novel "In Cold Blood") what Jamie Foxx did for **Ray**, in that his portrayal of the late, great Pulitzer Prize winning writer, **Truman Capote** is truly *chilling*. Hoffman doesn't play Capote - he is Capote! Without a doubt, best actor award at the 2006 Academy Awards. So convincing is he as a gay man, that his next role no doubt, will be "Homo Alone."

Rourke lands on rump! Ruckus making **Mickey Rourke** is headed for a fall! Not career-wise but literally a fall down on to the ground after getting decked by the boyfriend – half Rourke's size – of a girl he tries to romance in a night club. Before his bodyguards get to him, Mickey dukes it out with the kid, who is like greased lightening – far too young and strong – for the aging actor-turned-fighter to have much of a chance. Talented thespian though he be, Rourke needs a few lessons in humility and it's just a matter of time.... It'll be shades of **Frank Sinatra.** "Old blue eyes" got his "come upins" years ago in Las Vegas when he got punched out while surrounded by bodyguards after he tried to slug someone – another mobster – he greatly underestimated (... to say the least).

Hotel heiress queen **Paris Hilton** gets seriously hurt – or worse – in a boating or swimming mishap!... I "see" water skis, ramps and a fiery boat!

Legendary slap-stick funnyman **Jerry Lewis** does one more major television marathon for "Jerry's Kids" before calling it quits. A book and a big screen movie about his life with late partner and crooner extraordinaire **Dean Martin** will be a sensation in 2006. And well, he deserves it!

Former "Who's the Boss?" star **Tony Danza** is finally featured on the Biography Channel (A&E) after he's dumped from his current talk-show slot, goes ballistic and punches out two or three of the network bosses! (Tony was once a fighter.) Ironically it'll produce the intended effect of "high profile" since cops! guns! – and general mayhem will be involved! From this incident comes the call from Biography and offers to host new talk-shows, perhaps one called, ironically, – "Knock-Out!" Keep swinging, Tony, I see a great future for ya! (If he survives the brouhaha!)

Dustin Hoffman requires re-constructive surgery to his nose because Mrs.Hoffman threatens him with divorce for intolerable pain and suffering! He snores! Whoever worked on his schnozz last, failed to correct the deviated septum which sounds not unlike Shemp of "The Three Stooges," when he was asleep.

Hockey legend **Wayne Gretzky** is in for a series of bad luck – personally and professionally – not unlike that which **Conrad Black** (now in the *red*) is suffering.

Ironically "Bewitched" star **Nicole Kidman,** for all her healthy eating, will suffer the same disease – colon cancer! – that claimed the life of **Elizabeth Montgomery,** star of the original Bewitched TV series! Although diagnosed early and treated immediately, it nonetheless underlines the rumor that persons having anything to do with that old television series – and the current movie – are cursed! Thereafter bad luck seemed to dog their every move. Late actor **Dick York** who played the hapless husband of **Ms. Montgomery** on television, suffered a crippling back injury – right on set during filming – which rendered him helpless, immediately ending his career forever! He died years later in a charity ward for incurables, alone and penniless. The old series and this new movie have all the charm and "good fortune" as does "that Scottish Play" by Shakespeare whose name should never be mentioned while rehearsing or performing it... Macbeth! (– Psst... I'm not rehearsing or performing it, just printing it.)

Playboy empire chief **Hugh Hefner**.... You may take one long bunny hop right up to the Pearly Gates this year. ("May I?" "Yes, you may.")

Cutting wittster **Joan Rivers** to require new set of choppers when a burly former star of yesteryear pops her right in the kisser for rude remarks about her excess avoirdupois (weight). (Perhaps it's Babs Streisand?)

Believe-it-or-not! Beautiful **Sandra Bullock** tries to make he-man hubby **Jesse "Monster Garage" James** *her namesake* (and I don't mean by marrying him twice!), when she catches him "in the act" with a *monster* buxom blond – both buck naked – and attacks his crown jewels with a razor. Real cutting edge stuff that'll certainly make headlines!

Comedian **Eddie Murphy** is offered the juicy role of portraying the life and times of 70s television superstar funnyman **Flip "Geraldine" Wilson**, who also had a "thing" for transvestites. (Good old Eddie was pulled over by police late one night eight years ago with a transvestite prostitute in his car.) Also, Murphy will go on to greater cinematic acclaim when he undertakes the difficult job of dramatizing the life of the world's very first sex change recipient in the 1960s, **Christine Jorgenson**. (I suppose that would make it a dual role.) It will be the third remake of films previously done by white actors: Dr. Dolittle (Rex Harrison), The Nutty Professor (Jerry Lewis) and now Ms. Jorgenson. (Hmmmmm... "Miss Jorgenson"... not a bad title.)

Although **Dr. Phil** is now television's king of "pop psychology," this is a king who will send himself into exile! Too full of hubris and an incurable romantic at heart, dear Phillip will be caught in a compromising tryst involving female patients and their daughters! This spells *tout fini* for the "good" doctor's lucrative

career. What goes up, must come down – and anyone crazy enough to go see Dr. Phil should have his head examined!

Kim Bassinger and Alec Baldwin to reunite.

Oprah Winfrey becomes a HUGE success in Hollywood! After her network TV contract ends, she'll work behind the scenes to help produce progressive TV talk-shows, such as Dr. Phil or even spin-offs of self-help hits that bring her still more fame and fortune. A Nobel Prize, or an award from the Kennedy Center for the Performing Arts is definitely in her future.... I "see" it!

"Her Face Cracked the Mirror" star Barbara Streisand's problems are far from over. Even though she has recently faced down a cancer scare and packed on a whopping 30 lbs to her 5 ft. 5 in. frame because of career frustrations, Babs is (unknowingly) gearing up for an extended emotional roller coaster ride when she catches actor James Brolin, her handsome hunk-of-the-senior-set husband, screwing around with young starlets. This sends Babs over the edge and straight to the "funny farm" for R 'n' R. When eventually released she'll embark on a successful singing and lecture tour whose subject matter is "Living Life as a Fag Hag!" Her son, Jason Gould, is as "gay as a goose," and I don't mean happy. (*P.S. – Babs has just announced, as I reedit this, that she is going back on tour.)

London's original Madame Tussaud's wax museum will go up in flames! "Jewish lightening" will be blamed. (For those not "in the know," this means, "Strike a match for insurance, anyone?")

David Letterman will announce his retirement in 2006 due to heart and health problems in general. His temporary replacement will be a dark-haired woman, but for some reason this female late-night TV talk-show host is unable to cut it.

"Saving Private Ryan" star Tom Sizemore (or should that be *more size!*) is suffering from a rare and painful condition called priapism, in which the penis – namely *his* – stands permanently at attention – even after several consecutive un-interrupted romps in the sack (– including after climax!). The condition is usually caused by a combination of booze and medication (or drugs) and a mild form of the problem may come in handy, now and then. (Please allow this writer to brag a little in that I once had the same "problem," back in the day "while in my cups" *and* mixing alcohol with – whatever!) But in *extended* cases (–no pun intended –) amputation may be required because gangrene can set in. However, I predict in Mr. Moresize's case – uh, I mean, Mr. Sizemore's case – the problem will resolve itself naturally when the talented actor *rises* to the occasion by getting his act together. Keep a *stiff* upper lip, Tom – uh, I mean, keep a... well, – you know what I mean....

Actor **Verne Troyer**, who played Dr. Evil's thirty-two inch alter ego "Mini-Me" in the Austin Powers movies, is feeling *low* because of his recent divorce from now ex-wife **Genevieve Gallen**. "I'm so down," said the tiny thespian, "that I have to jump up just to reach bottom." (...Ouch!) Although I predict he'll move on to *bigger* and better things, career wise, I'm sorry to say I see a tragic end for the drinking dwarf, from one too many battles with the bottle.

Record producer **Phil Spector** will complete the terrible "triumvirate of marriage murderers" who have escaped the noose when he is acquitted of killing the poor lass who allegedly shot *herself* in the face! (Just like Pope Paul I, who suddenly "died in his sleep" right after his inaugural speech when he announced he was going to investigate "all that missing money from Vatican bank accounts;" or like their banker who "committed "suicide" by hanging himself from a bridge in London, weighted down with bricks in his pockets and his hands tied behind his back! Yeah, right. (Suicide, Italian style!)

Pamela Anderson suffers major health setbacks as a result of her Hep-C which will directly impact on her liver, leading to fatal or near-fatal consequences.

Soon only one little Beatle will be left, as the penultimate one is squashed by father time. ("...one little, two little, three little Indians...")

Although **Farrah Fawcett** is now a Hollywood turn off (– "Faw-cett," "turn off" – "Turn off faucet?" – get it?), she'll make a spectacular comeback as a touring seniors fitness guru, traveling across America visiting wealthy retirement homes and lecturing on the value of moderate exercise. I see her starring in a weekly television show based on all this stuff. "C'mon! Work out with Charlie's Angel," may well be the marketing slogan.

LaToya Jackson, whose only real talent – let's face it – is in being her brother **Michael's** sister. As she ages, Ms. Jackson will – like Michael – begin to rely far too much on plastic surgery to keep that other minor talent, her *looks,* from fade–fade–fading away, until – horror of horrors! – she ends up resembling a terror stricken banshee! It won't be long before she follows her late husband, **Jack Gordon**, down into Sheol (Hebrew underworld, abode of the dead).

Truly the *only* real 007 is **Sean Connery**, who'll make "just one more" James Bond movie, no matter how often he denies it. I predicted to **Sylvester Stallone** that he would star in "just one more" Rocky and Rambo movie, which he is. (...Hmm – Rocky & Rambo ...sounds like a pair of tough cartoon characters.)

Rod "gravel voice" **Stewart** may have failed miserably trying his hand at singing old standards, but a whole new career in Hollywood films lies before him as the new Godfather to replace that beloved voice portrayed by the late **Marlon Brando**. "...Un-n-n, Michael, my son... You papa loves-a-you, ver-ra much-a."

Charleze Theron, thinking she may never top her MONSTER Oscar-winning performance – is once more struck by tragedy while searching for another perfect role. Once again she survives and trumps her nemesis by utilizing the experience to win even greater acclaim! I see more blood and violence around her! – Yes, it could be just another movie about her early life. However I do believe that this *is* a *two-part* vision that *must come to pass!*

Larry Hagman finds religion a solace for his troubled life, which brings him peace in this, his twilight years. (*Is* that "twilight" – or just a reflection of light filtering through the bottom of his wine glass?)

William "Captain Kirk" **Shatner** truly finds his niche in TV when he takes on the role of a priest (or minister) in a city neighborhood akin to New York's Hell's Kitchen! Set in the aftermath of a catastrophic terrorist attack, the series expands from there. Key word – success!

Toby "Spiderman" **McGuire** is so stereotyped that his

chances of returning to the screen as a serious actor are between zip and zilch! However he'll eventually escape this humiliating experience when he accepts the role of lithium-besotted creative genius, Toronto born Glen Gould, whose state of mind Toby most resembles anyway!

Clint Eastwood will own up to being the son of late comic genius **Stan Laurel,** of "Laurel and Hardy" fame.

Canadian Ambassador **Mike Myers** continues to promote Toronto and Canada in his next three movies, which are set in the glamorous period of Hollywood's Golden Era (the 1940s), even though Hollywood North – Toronto – stands in for old Tinsletown.

Blind Toronto Blues musician/club owner **Jeff Healy** will thank his lucky stars when fifty percent of his vision is restored in one eye! This takes the skilled guitarist to new heights. ("... and in the land of the blind, the one-eyed man was king!")

New information forthcoming that "old blue eyes" **Frank Sinatra** had first-hand knowledge of **Marilyn Monroe's** and **John F. Kennedy's** murders! (Possibly by Chicago mobster San Giancona)

As a former rumpologist (reading celebrity butts!) **Jacqueline Stallone** and I have always said that crotch-grabbing **Roseanne Barr** has a great *future "behind"* her! She'll be well on her way back up the glass mountain in 2006!

Jackie Mason, a comic genius on stage but an obnoxious s.o.b. off, will be charged with profanity after an extremely repugnant remark made to the wife of a prominent politician, who is also a sitting judge! Mason will appear in court sporting very dark "sunglasses," sans rims!

Oscar-winning actress **Glenda Jackson** to rise much higher than the political office she currently holds in the Labor Party, even unto the Prime Minister's office itself!

Fugitive film maker **Roman Polanski** will be granted full pardon. This marks his return to Hollywood!

Julia Roberts suffers a life threatening infection when a plastic surgery procedure goes terribly wrong! Anaphylactic shock! – but she ultimately pulls through.

Dustin Hoffman stars in a fabulous new film about the life and times of the "old schnozzla" himself, Jimmy Durante. And with a beak like that – how can he miss! He already looks like a tired anteater.

Madonna receives death threats when she goes Country & Western. (Oh – my stars! Me think the lady doth go to far!) Will she sing, "Don't Cry for Me Argentina" – through her adenoids? Heaven forbid! No wonder the death threats!... I see a cowboy hat, boots, spurs – the whole nine yards!

Rosie O'Donnel to head up a lesbian commune. But again, she invites enmity that causes her relationships to suffer. She seems to open her mouth only to change feet. This time it'll be different. This time she'll open her mouth to firmly insert *both* feet!

Keith Richards and **Sir Mick Jagger** are electrocuted on stage during an outdoor concert in the rain. Whether it's caused by lightening or their axes (guitars) or both simultaneously, the end result is the same – death!

Susan Sarandon and hubby **Tim Robbins** find themselves on the proverbial "S--- list" and their once prestigious careers in shambles when they are viewed as traitors and Quislings and placed on a new Hollywood blacklist!

James Gandolfini of the Sopranos hit series has become overweight and his friends are now calling him "fat-fella" instead of good-fella! Serious health problems, but as soon as he meets his new love – a statuesque blonde – his weight'll drop dramatically due to sudden "exercise."

Wayne Newton, Mr. Las Vegas, will serve jail time for alleged tax evasion. The problem is he really does not owe Uncle Sam and the IRS the cool $1.8 million they claim, at least not according to Newton's accountants. I predict that on principle alone "he'll do the time" 'til the tax boys admit their mistake – publicly – and release him. Don't hold your breath, Wayne – and for God's sake keep your butt tight up against the bars! Even at your age you're gonna look pretty good to some of those guys! (Trust me on this one!)

Ex-jailbird **Stacy Keach** will reprise his role as a convict. (In 1984 he was imprisoned in Reading Jail, England, and served nine months for importing an ounce of coke from France. And I don't Coca-Cola – although cocaine *was* once a part of its original recipe!) Once again he will be picked-up by police and charged with possession, but this time it turns out to be only a publicity stunt to promote his new Fox TV series Prison Break – for which he does serve a little time after ticking off the police who charge him with public mischief.

Whether **Drew Barrymore** – last of the great Barrymores – is gay or not is not the issue. The fun-lovin' actress will soon be "pregers," if for no other reason than to offer up yet another link to join the chain of that illustrious family. A boy!

"The Long Kiss Goodbye" star **Geena Davis** is doing just that to her long movie career as she segues from big screen to mini-screen, which is to say television. Ms. Davis will be featured in a home-cookin'-type show on which she takes up with a young, blond Adonis half her age – on and off camera! ... Must be careful of fire in her house, where I see pets – dogs, cats – rescued before it burns to the ground!

Clueless" star **Alicia Silverstone**, looking slightly pregnant, will give birth to twin boys! If not by the first deposit than certainly by the second, for I "see" three children– a girl and twin boys – and then divorce! Her husband, rock musician **Chris Jarecki**, will want to escape the chains of matrimony to have a gay, old time... After all, he writes poetry, or didn't ya know?

One right after the other, **Andy Griffith** and **Don Knotts** (of "Mayberry") will pass away within a week or two of each other. Their departure from this realm to the Electrical One will encourage Las Vegas to make book on "who goes first," even going so far as to give odds on the "spread" of days between them.

Courtney Love, much publicized misfit, falls into a state of disrepair that leaves her fighting for her life, on this her last downward and fatal spiral into the abyss.... Some people can't be helped, can't help themselves, are simply doomed....

Angelina Jolie is a "mad woman," says ex-hubby **Billy Bob Thornton**, in a tell-all exposé His revealing autobiography, depicting the tumultuous relationship she and he had, will leave her livid as she physically attacks "Davey Crockett" at popular Hollywood restaurant, MATTEOS.

Mel Gibson creates his own Australian movie studios – dwarfing all other giants – thus becoming huge, even by Hollywood standards!

Antonio Banderas and **Melanie Griffith** are headed for the "last round-up," at least marriage wise. A drug overdose by one of the children leaves the couple in shock, unable to cope, followed by separation... then again, reconciliation, since one of the truest sayings of all time is "misery loves company."

Octogenarian **Kirk Douglas**, married 50 years, shows no signs of retiring. Blockbuster movies keep rolling in and he'll "die with his boots on" – literally – while portraying a cowboy.

Million Dollar Baby" Oscar winner **Hilary Swank** stars in a new (and old) vehicle which sees her garner yet another Oscar. It's the remake of tragic 1930s movie icon **Francis Farmer**, the blond beauty whose battle with insanity was more legendary than her talents as an actress, which were considerable. In the end, it seems her conflict was over her suppressed (or repressed) lesbian nature. Toward the end of her life, Francis did pursue a successful gay relationship with the woman who encouraged her to write the best-selling autobiography, "Will There Ever be a Morning?" ...Hillary! Take a page.

Michelle Pfeiffer ("WOLF") will head up a hugely successful cola company (I "see" bottles filled with brown liquid) of which she'll be the big shot, big cheese – in short, head honcho. I "see" her moving further and further away from movies to money – really **BIG, BIG MONEY!** She'll take up with an industrialist from Europe who is – unfortunately – a munitions manufacturer and a shipping magnate.

Marc Anthony, husband of singer **J. Lo,** will be arrested for striking his wife in public!

Robert Redford, Hollywood icon actor/director, will be honored with a Lifetime Achievement Award by the film industry – possibly at the Lincoln Center for the Performing Arts – for his long time contributions to the encouragement of independent film making. But right at the apex of his acclaim, a nasty sex scandal, involving this talented and giving man – erupts, forcing him to publicly defend his good name. A real cause célèbre – attracting world-wide attention! (...which is what "cause célèbre" means, doesn't it?).

Show biz legend **Carol Channing** to pass away. But no one's the wiser! Her good friend, a female impersonator, carries on *in her shoes* – literally— performing as Channing! And it'll last quite some time before the fraud is discovered! It may be said, in **Mark Twain**'s words, – if Carol were capable of uttering them from the grave: "Rumors of my death have been greatly exaggerated!"

News that "Back to the Future" star **Michael J. Fox** is losing his battle with Parkinson's, the disease which struck him at the height of his career! But I predict a revolutionary treatment – now in the doorway of discovery – will halt and reverse the condition – and that of *all* sufferers of this dreaded disease.

Elizabeth Taylor, 74, becomes a mom again! Her role as an adoptive parent will leave her exhausted and certainly with no time for her own role as Queen of Hollywood society.... So what's the harm if it keeps her young and motivated? Plus its good for the kid, which is the main thing.

Magnum P.I.'s **Tom Sellick** will be featured on the world-wide-web exposing all in a steamy threesome! And then the world discovers he's not such an "Aww, shucks" nice guy, after all.

Hollywood bad boy **Stephen Baldwin** claims he has rediscovered his faith: "Since 9/11 I think God has put me in a position so that I can have a voice with which to speak to a certain culture" When confronted by hellish Muslim extremists, this causes him to falter and re-think his public declaration of faith....Oh ye, of little faith!

Country star **Kenny Rogers'** wife worries that recent Rogers' recordings will lead her young twins astray. She's right on with this premonition! Not only will Rogers' "hootin' and hollerin'" send the twins (Jordan and Justin) down the wrong road, they're going to become a "bad to the bone" country duo, to boot!

Val Kilmer is packing on pounds! If he continues taking on "avoir du pois," the once teen heart-throb "Batman" will have to consider the risks of overeating in order to see the next five years –

else he's looking at a *permanent* early retirement. A *grave* situation!

Multi-tycoon **Martha Stewart** has death breathing down her neck. A severe case of bad nerves mixed with cocaine suddenly causes her to collapse. And it's nearly fatal!

A close friend of **George Clooney** suffers a fatality in rough waters – perhaps even George himself! This presents George, or his estate, with another headache – a lawsuit!

Hillary Clinton will sweep to political victory in a campaign that puts her up yet another rung on her bid to become America's first female president, certainly at least vice-president.

"Coal-miner's daughter" **Loretta Lynn** wins another music award before she cashes in (her blue stock chips).

Ernest Borgnine, star of "MARTY" and "McHale's Navy," is still working at 87 and still will be at 99! This charismatic actor has the gift of longevity in his career and in his life and will probably pass the 100 mark. Lifetime achievement award coming for Old Borgie – and I do mean *"old."* He will be supremely feted!

The gay world is shaken to its pink (or is that fuchsia?) foundation when a very high profile member of their community is horribly murdered! As a result, new U.S. and Canadian Laws are enacted to ensure future commensurate punishment for such acts of persecution and brutality.

Madonna – pop diva, mother and author of a successful line of children's books – will snap! When the stress of constantly being scrutinized by the public mixes with the stress of child-rearing, Madonna will forever swear off children, and in a new book urge all potential mothers to seriously consider abortion! The book places Madonna in the "bad books" of the Catholic Church, to say the least.

Jacqueline Stallone

Astrologer Extraordinaire
Writer / Lecturer

January 2005

As an astrologer and author ("STAR POWER: AN ASTROLOGICAL GUIDE TO SUPER SUCCESS!" – PUBLISHER, NEW AMERICAN LIBRARY), and after meeting and talking with virtually every psychic on this continent and in Europe – including the late Jean Dixon – et all, I'm truly and deeply impressed by the extraordinary gifts of the Toronto psychic-palmist, Anthony Carr.

Anthony is gifted paranormally in a virtually unique way. I say unique because where other psychics, seers, clairvoyants, telepathists – and, believe me – I've met them all – Tony   gets bizarre psychic images that have proved amazingly accurate! His ability to see into the future is eerie, to say the least.

In plain English, Tony sees the future. He really does!!! Many of his predictions are seen on television, radio, and have been recorded in print around the world – long before the events occurred!

I think you can get a great item out of Anthony by playing up the angle, "the man who sees the future" *before* the event – not after, as most people do.

I am writing this letter as a favor to Anthony. However, I certainly would not vouch for him if he were not good. I think my record as being honest stands on its own merit, around the world. He is uniquely gifted. He truly sees the future! I have worked with Anthony on numerous shows, world wide.

Sincerely,

Jacqueline Stallone

Hands of Destiny

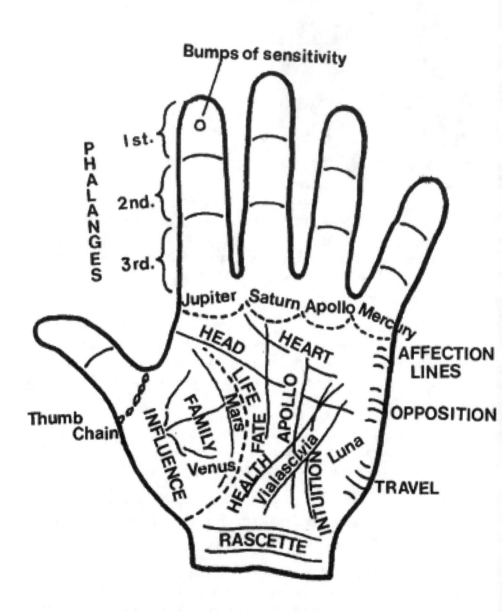

Bumps of sensitivity

PHALANGES

1st.

2nd.

3rd.

Jupiter Saturn Apollo Mercury

HEAD HEART

AFFECTION LINES

LIFE

FAMILY INFLUENCE

Mars

FATE

APOLLO

OPPOSITION

Thumb Chain

Venus

HEALTH

Vialasciyia

Intuition

Luna

TRAVEL

RASCETTE

LINES & MOUNTS

JACQUELINE STALLONE

Even though "Jackie," famed astrologer and mother of super-star actor Sylvester Stallone, worked hard to become independently wealthy enough to insist Sly hold out for the starring lead in his own screenplay (the first Rocky), she also has in her hand all the configurations of a child who will catapult his parents onto the world stage!

Look just below her fourth or Mercury finger and see all the little influence lines, sweeping up from the Heartline and merging with the children lines. And then the Apollo line appearing and growing stronger directly beneath the third finger of the same name, but above the Heartline, indicating great success – but late in life!

I predict Jacqueline Stallone will soon become the darling of European aristocracy through her accurate planetary prognostications. I also see a highly successful television show – beamed around the world! She'll also become a mother again! (Through adoption?)

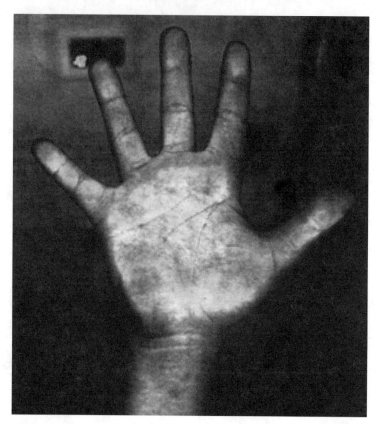

SYLVESTER "ROCKY" STALLONE

Sly has a strong, powerful hand which mostly resembles the talented Earth hand, in that it's a very square palm with somewhat short fingers. He has a long first or Jupiter finger – longer then the third – indicating a "take charge" kind of guy. He has only the four basic lines (Life- Head- Heart- and Fatelines) which allow for "straight ahead" concentration, as opposed to a hand with a profusion of lines covering it, as in his mother's hand, which can lead to nervous exhaustion as a result of too much Electrical Energy coursing through the body.

In the near future, Sylvester must guard his health, moderation being the key word here. He'll need to conserve energy because he'll be moving ahead by leaps and bounds – literally! New Rambo and Rocky flicks in his future! (* Predicted last June in 2004 addition of STARGAZER.)

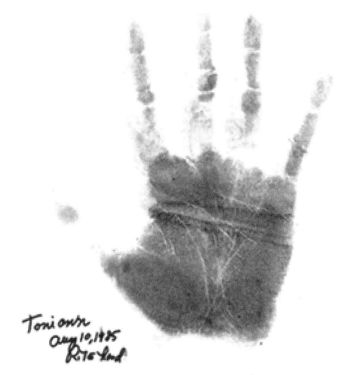

Toni onn
aug 10, 1985
Rio Land

TONI-ANN, SYLVESTER'S SISTER

Toni-Ann possesses the Square or business hand (which is a Square palm with *definite* long fingers). These people are "usually" well-organized, with their lives planned well ahead.

A Square hand should possess only the 4 basic lines (Life- Head- Fate- and Heartlines), which give them great powers of concentration and organization. Unfortunately, Toni-Ann's palm is covered with a profusion of lines, like a spider's web, which go off in all directions at once (– if I may borrow a line from from a Dylan Thomas poem –) but get nowhere!

Her luck over the past few years has not been so good because of this tendency to dash off everywhere simultaneously, but her Fate-line and Apollo line begin to "straighten out and fly right" as she approaches that period in her life when reason takes precedent over emotion.

I see nothing but great good luck and a brand new man in her brand new Future! (Or a brand new relationship with her current one... – a gold band?)

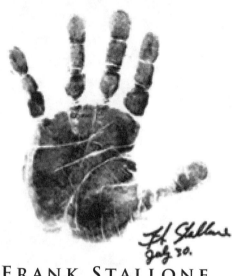

FRANK STALLONE

A very talented actor and musician (composer of musical soundtrack for Rocky I) who starred in the film "Barfly," playing the bartender who was always fist fighting with Mickey Rourke's character, Henry Chinaski, based on the real-life story of Charles Bukowski – poet and journalist – who spent his life as a drunken writer and brawler in sleazy bars in L.A, wherein he died.

Possessing a hand similar to his brother, it is more of the Fire hand-type (long palm, short fingers). This signals someone who is impulsive, intuitive and sees the overall picture but cannot stand the actual work of piecing together the picture, preferring to leave the details to his longer-fingered brethren. Look at this powerful Mount of Venus (that high fleshy part just inside the lifeline, at the bottom of the thumb. This Mount is ruled by Venus and is indicative of a voluptuary, one who loves all things Venusian – good food, good wine, bad women and song. (Not necessarily in that order.)

If you look at his Fateline (the line running straight up the center of the palm, ending under the Saturn or second finger), you will see that it becomes much thicker and stronger after the age of 50, or so, just above the Heartline. There is no doubt that his greatest successes are about to begin, and he will achieve his heart's desire – in every way, shape and form....I "see" a wedding band and a petite little blonde – very beautiful! – coming his way. (And if I'm wrong – sue me!)

ELLA FITZGERALD

She was the apotheosis of a Fire hand (short fingers, long palm). "Ella," as she was known to her intimates, was moody – temperamental, creative (slopping Headline(s)) – but extremely giving of her time and money – especially where children and orphanages were concerned. You will note the double line of Head, one below the other. This indicates extra brain power and a dual personality, which she often exhibited: one being extreme self-confidence while on stage, and the other shyness and self-effacement – almost self-loathing – when off!

She had a much-rayed palm, with lines covering the entire surface, which would normally cause its owner to scatter her forces due to the excess energy – particularly when it is accompanied by a weak thumb. But in Ella's case, the scattered lines were deeply etched, allowing better control of the emotions (or Energy), plus she had a powerful thumb for control, as well.

Of course when I last looked at her hands, she asked if she would ever marry again (she being at the time between husbands), and I replied, "Although you still have several 'flings' ahead of you, your time would be better spent pursuing your favorite charities."

As she was leaving, she looked over her shoulder, and said: "Hmmm...should I look for a house near a school?" She truly did love children.

JOHHNY DEPP

An extremely sensitive hand, Mr. Depp's palm reminds me of a delicately constructed electrical instrument, in that the least little upset can throw the current (or the individual) out of whack! Even the bony structure of the hand itself (called chirognomy) is fitted together in such a way as to indicate translucency, not to mention the fine, thread-like, arachnoid meshwork of lines crisscrossing the entire hand proper.

This individual has abundant – but scattered – Electrical Energy which must find an outlet – or explode! The restlessness is compounded by the rather wide space between the head- and Life-lines, right beneath the first (or Jupiter) finger and immediately tells of someone who acts before he thinks, usually getting into trouble because he didn't listen to his instincts but would rather think "logically" instead of intuitively, especially with that long straight, Head line that indicates an above-average-intelligence. These longer Headlines are usually too cerebral, instead of relying on gut instincts, as people with very short Headlines do.

Soon, Depp will be called on to portray the life of a priest, exactly who I'm not certain. But one thing I am certain of, he should never again take on the role of an historical figure who has a checkered past, as he did in portraying the life of Peter Pan creator, Sir J.M. Barrie, "The Lost Boys" and "Searching for Neverland."

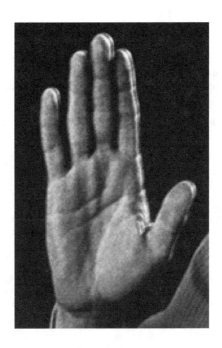

LEONARDO

The Aviator star has a typical Fire hand (long palm, short fingers) which signals an impulsive but intuitive individual who truly gets by on intuition, "sees" the whole picture when he "strategizes" – but utterly loathes detail work, preferring to let his long-fingered counterpart do the minutiae. Short finger's motto is –"Let's conquer the world – but you take care of the details!"

This "Catch Me If You Can" actor holds his fingers close together and tells me he is very good at keeping secrets – and his money! (Very straight Headline, practical and logical.) In fact, I'll bet the last time this guy took a buck out of his pocket – Washington blinked at the light and had to wear sunglasses! DiCaprio probably throws money around like Venus by the Dimilo...throws quarters around like manhole covers! Am I making my point here? I mean, – this _is_ a cheap guy!...So tight, he actually *squeaks* when he walks!

I predict Leonardo DiCaprio will learn a few lessons in humility, when the father of a little girl who wants his autograph, knocks him on his keester for demanding payment from the heartbroken child! Plus, there is danger for the Titanic star around water, not on film – but for real, not reel!

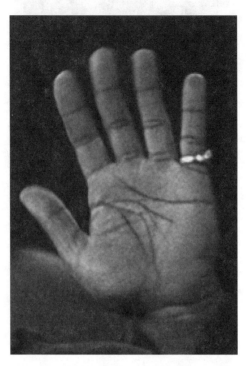

ICE CUBE

Actor-Rapper singer Ice Cube has a classic Earth hand, in that he lives and thrives through his basic instinct. The hand is short, thick and stocky in appearance and betrays an individual who enjoys working with his hands (music, building – punching out people, for instance). But it also indicates a sympathetic nature, one on whom a "sob story" (true or not) can go a long way – if you play it right (deep, sympathetic Heartline). However, the space between the Heartline and Headline is rather narrow and signals some selfishness – especially regarding his career (Headline humps up toward Heartline, creating narrow space, and he is, by nature, a take-charge kind of guy (all fingers lean toward first finger of Jupiter, which says: – "Do as I say, not as I do!" The good strong thumb (willpower and determination) will take him a long way; strong Venus Mount says he loves his comforts but that he always champions the underdog (or should that be "underdawg, y'all).

I predict Mr. Cube will go a long way, career wise I "see" him lying or living on an island but he must guard against high blood pressure and injury to the head, because of a volatile nature.

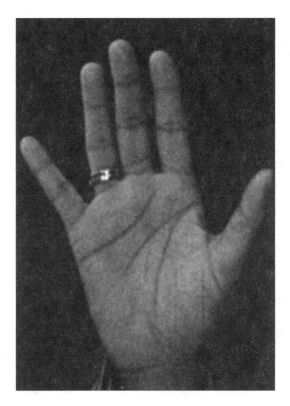

WHITNEY HOUSTON
($$$ CASH CRASH)

Troubles with hubby Bobby Brown are etched on her palms. The grid pattern on Whitney's Mount of Venus reveals great talent, but big personal problems. A cash crash is coming. Whitney will lose a fortune in bad investments. A close female pal will help her bounce back. She'll advise Whitney to replace bad boy Bobby with a rich husband who won't drain her fortune."

The fact that her baby or Mercury finger stands aloof from the rest, signals a cry for a attention and recognition. She, believe it or not, will be offered a golden oppurtunity to get into BIG TIME real estate investment, that pays off handsomely - not only financially - but handsomely as in a brand new baeu! Good luck, Whitney.

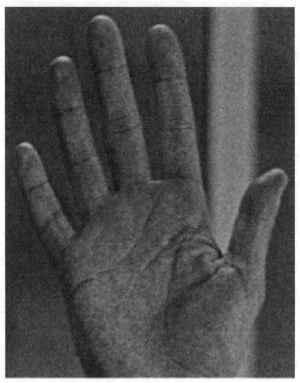

JUDE LAW

A very emotional restrictive nature is shown in Mr. Law's hand. (Lifeline too much restricting the Venus Mount instead of sweeping out into a nice wide arch to the center of the hand.) Because of this, people might accuse him of being emotionally distant. Worse, his Heartline is "frayed" (like a frayed electrical wire), and although he can be erratic (as in a wire that's not carrying the current properly because it's damaged), for the most part he is under control (strong thumbs-up).

Eventually though, he will explode...I "see" him in trouble with the law involving a terrible sex scandal! The world soon learns of Jude Law's not so charming side when he gets into an altercation with police who (– wait for it! –) charge him with ..."improper use of a public facility, in one of the stalls of the "Men's" room! (Hmmm....Shades of Sir John Gielgud!)

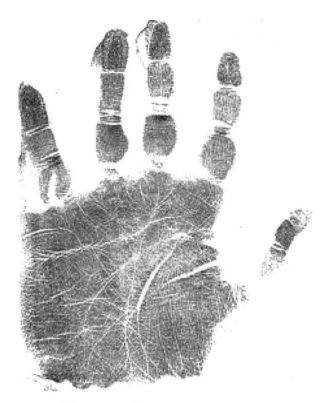

PAUL BERNARDO
(CHILD KILLER)
THE DEVIL'S HAND!

This is the hand of the sexually violent sadist Paul Bernardo, and his accomplice "Judas goat" wife, Karla Holmolka, who tortured, raped, killed and dismembered St. Catherine's area schoolgirls Leslie Mahaffy and Kristen French.

As you can see, the hand is broad and strong and primitive (– "primitive" used here in its negative sense as in "brutish!"), with a profusion of incredibly fine lines completely covering the palm, indicating no control of the life Energy whatsoever and exacerbated by the short, almost truncated fingers. Even the four main lines: Head- Heart- Life- and Fate are not solidly incised in the hand but are weak and fuzzy showing no emotional or mental strength of "control." This monster acts on every impulse – plus the low-set thumb, with its weak nail tip, is not nearly strong enough to control these impulses. Bernardo will die in prison – not of old age – but by the "general population," when a prison riot breaks out and they drag the scum out of his cage and give him what he deserves.

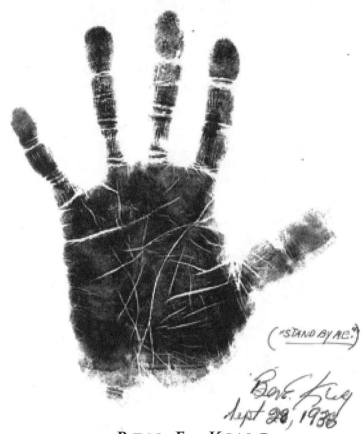

(*"STAND BY ME."*)

BEN E. KING

(Composer /Vocalist of perinea /favorite, "Stand by me")

    I first met "Ben E.," as we all called him, many (many!) years ago when I was wearing my other "hat" as a saxophone player and briefly worked for him. I then studied his hand (also of the Fire type) and told him: "years from now – this was the mid '60s when he was still at the top of the game – when you are in a slump, someone is going to take one of your "old" records and re-release it, and this will revive your career – taking you to undreamed of heights.

    And sure enough decades later, when he was in a bit of a slump, Hollywood caught on to one of his (now) "old" records, "Stand By Me," and used it as the signature song for the hit movie of the same name. It catapulted him on to the world stage – making him a bigger star then he was previously. An ever thoughtful as ever Ben E. sent me a nice letter to remind me of what I had prophesied, to these many long years ago!

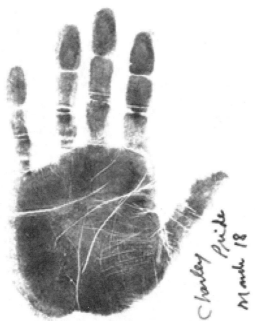

CHARLEY PRIDE

Once upon a time long ago Charley Pride came through on tour. I was playing sax in a 1950's Rock & Roll band ("Ronnie G. and the G-men") divey bar, the St. Louis (Ronnie also owned the joint), w-a-a-a-y up in Northern Ontario, Canada (a thousand miles from any other place!) in a town called Thunder Bay (formally named Fort William and Port Arthur), where only loggers, truckers and Indians (Native Canadians) came to drink. The place was so rough that even the two bouncers – the "town toughs" – used to fight each other out of boredom, on slow nights.

The local paper sends me out to cover the concert and in his dressing room we sat for an hour and I took a look at his palms: "Charley," I said. "The most salient points in your palm are the nicely sloping Headline (romantic creativity) and the fact that it starts inside the Lifeline, high up on the Jupiter Mount, beneath the finger of the same name (which is shorter than the third finger, of Apollo, indicates a slight inferiority complex, which exist only in your mind, no one else's." He said, "Wazzat, you say?... I think you're right."

At any rate I had cause to talk about him recently with an old friend of his (actually Barry Haugen, editor of this book) and looking at that old print, I said "I have a strong feeling that he is poised for a big comeback...." We shall see if "time" proves me right.

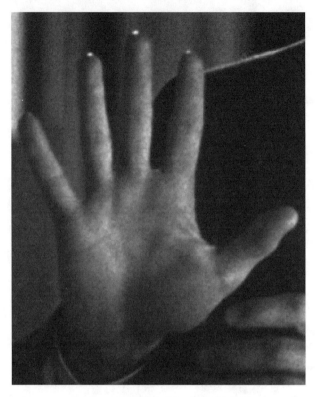

TOM CRUISE

Finely etched lines reflect sensitivity and intelligence – as well as a weak life force. Formally wed to actress Nicole Kidman, the longtime Scientologist will soon arrive at a critical crossroads –yet again! Tom will be hit by a new kind "love," like a lightning bolt and deal with it badly. His religious faith will be shaken –but he'll never really leave Nicole –not really, especially emotionally. He will always be tied to her, that way. Instead he's about to make major life changes that will eventually bring him greater happiness.

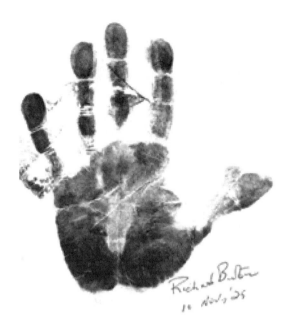

RICHARD BURTON

Many people have asked me what the later, great, rambunctious actor Richard Burton was like? My reply always is: – "He was just like any other normal man, only more so."

Being a Scorpio person, by Sun sign, he was obsessed with death and "the meaning of life," and all that.
"...Quite frankly," he once told me, "I suppose I'm really an agnostic," as he looked at me quizzically, to see if I knew what the word meant, for to ask me directly, I suppose, would have seemed like an insult. I assured him I knew what it meant (barely), and replied, "Maybe the answer is – there is no answer."

He held out his hand and asked me point-blank how much longer he had to live? Since we are taught to "tap dance" around such sensitive issues as death, I "hemmed and hawed" a little, but he insisted on knowing (being a Scorpio) and so I said, "I can't know for certain, but as I look at your hollow palm, I can 'see' you will first have to be reunited with your former wife, Elizabeth Taylor – whom you twice married! – in full view of the media, and shortly after that you will go down hill rapidly." Although at the time he was married to Susan Hunt, upon hearing that Elizabeth was to appear in the popular stage play, "The Little Foxes," at the Old Vic in London, he immediately flew to be by her side, and shortly after succumbed.

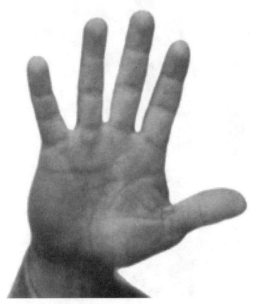

ARNOLD SCHWARZENEGGER

Arnie, der "Terminator/ Govern-ator," possesses an almost pure Spatulate hand (very broad at the base and narrow at the top) with fairly long fingers. It belongs to people with robust health and driving ambition, especially in the areas of "boldly going where no one has gone before." This is the hand of an adventurer and explorer who'll be the first to plunge into an unexplored forest – but then you'll have to send in a rescue party to bring him out!

Trouble is, such a muscular hand should go...ahem, "hand in hand" with strong lines to carry correctly throughout the body the Electrical Energy – otherwise known as the Life force. Not so in Governor Arnie's case: the lines are faint and weak and is one of the reasons he suffered near-fatal heart problems several years ago, when I read his palms at the Toronto premier of the Christmas film "Jingle All The Way" and predicted he would be hospitalized with a serious cardiac problem. I reported my palmist findings to the Globe in Florida and the Toronto Sun. Three months later, the unthinkable happened. He was wheeled into the hospital and underwent emergency heart value replacement surgery – not once – but twice within four hours! The first one failed to work properly.

I predict this California Governor will fail miserably, return to "acting" temporarily before once again making a bid for the White House – successfully!...But remember, those German roots run deep!

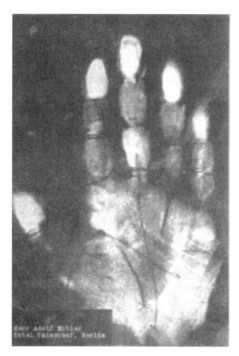 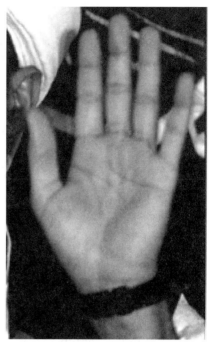

ADOLPH HITLER / BIN LADEN

In this only existing photograph of Herr Hitler's hand it is evident that his perverted genius was due in part to a misdirected libido. Actually terrorist madman Osama Bin Laden and diabolical Nazi Adolph Hitler go "hand in hand" when it comes to evil!

Hitler's mitt is of the creative elementary – that is, short rounded fingers atop a square palm; but the palm rises from beneath a very low-set Mercury or baby finger, signposting problems in relationships with women (to say the least), up to a high set Jupiter, or dominating – even tyrannical – personality. His hand is the heavier and thicker of the two, indicating materialistic ambitions while bin Laden's hand, more delicately constructed but with a slightly sloping Headline, is far more idealistic, romantic, and certainly "more creative," therefore his burning ambition is driven by his notion of ideology, of what's right or wrong. But make no bones about it – both are fanatics! By the way, Hitler is more the Air-hand type – square palm, long fingers – while bin Laden is of the Fire-type (short fingers atop a long palm).

So, in summing up: The shape of their thumbs: – Hitler with a strong well-developed thumb, whose tip is wider at its base, won't tolerate opposition. Bin Laden's thumbs are not as "manly" and developed as "the Fuhrers, indicating at heart he's a coward.

Their palms: – Hitler's thick, square palm and average-length finger indicate incredible egocentricity. Bin Laden's is more delicate, narrower and longer, indicating sensitivity and nervousness. (And well he should be!)

Their fingers: – Both men's pinkies are longer and straighter than average with long, rounder – verging on pointed – tips, indicating great persuasiveness in speech making. Both have Jupiter fingers (first) that are more or less pointed, indicating a consuming desire to rule people. But Hitler's extra long Jupiter finger (longer then his third) indicates supreme confidence (even when it's not warranted). And bin Laden has a shorter first finger, indicating a raging insecurity.

Their Headlines (The palm's middle line): – Hitler's strong Headline shows the will to lead, and did lead through sheer brute force! – while bin Laden's line "trails off," showing self-delusion and the ability to lead "delicately," through emotional manipulation, the demagogue, that he is.

Their Lifelines: – (The line curving around the Mount of Venus, at the base of the thumb.) The good news is that bin Laden is not destined to live much longer. His Lifeline terminates at nearly the same point as Hitler's, who committed suicide in Nazi, Germany at age 56. (We should be so lucky!)

The Mystery of the Haunted Bed_____

Part I

A Haunted Bed?

Ridiculous you say?

Well, there are haunted houses, haunted caves and haunted ships – so why not a 150 year-old bed? Read the tale of Mary Milne of Toronto, Ontario in Canada.

Mary with Headboard

Mary, an attractive young divorcee with two teenage daughters, was a career woman and, after what she described as three years of terror, seems nonetheless to be reasonably happy.

She was returning home from a late night party early in 1975. This was the beginning of the nightmare which nearly drove her out of her mind.

"…Walking from my car to the elevator," Mary recalled, "something made me glance at the far corner of the underground parking lot. That's when I first saw the bed. It was beautiful and appeared to have been abandoned.

"I dragged the bed up to my apartment, assembled it and stood back to admire my handiwork. It was gorgeous and very old. Why anyone would throw away something so valuable was beyond me.

"I was studying the bed when this weird, very chilling sensation came over me. Blaming it on fatigue I got ready for my bath and decided that next morning I would buy a mattress and make this lovely old be my own. This was the greatest mistake of my life.

"I ordered the mattress and that night when my daughter and I were asleep in the bed something caused me to sit bolt upright. There at the foot of the bed stood my best girlfriend. He lips were moving but there was no sound.

I remember glancing at the clock. It was 2:03 a.m., and I said: 'Marian, what on earth are you doing here at this hour?'

"She didn't answer and I began to think I was hallucinating. Then Heather woke up and asked: 'Who are you talking to, Mother? Mother! What's that blue light at the end of the bed?' Then Marian, or her apparition – disappeared.

"Neither my daughter or I could get back to sleep so we got up.

"While we were sitting at the kitchen table, there was a furious knock at the door. With great apprehension I opened the door to find two burly policemen standing there:

'Are you Mary Milne?'

'Yes'

'Do you know a Marian Ducet?'

'Yes, I do.'

'Well I'm sorry to have to tell you this, but she's just been murdered.'

"I was in such a state of shock I could hardly understand what they were saying.

"The police said Marian was walking from her car when a man lunged from the shadows and bludgeoned her to death with a monkey wrench.

"The man lived in our building. Later when interviewed by the press he stated (and this is on record): I don't know what came over me, it's as though I was possessed.'

"He occupied the apartment above me. Marian had lived directly over him – and was murdered right below my place *at the very spot where I had found the bed.*

"After the police left I was exhausted, and began to doze off when I suddenly jumped to my feet. I was sure I felt the bed *trembling!* I didn't say anything about this to anyone. People would naturally attribute it to nerves.

"There was something strange about that bed. Who had thrown it out in the first place? And why? Although I hadn't mentioned the trembling in the bed to my daughters, neither of them would sleep in it. My youngest, who wanted to sleep in it, ran from the bedroom screaming: 'Someone's laughing at me from under the bed."

"This was only the first in a chain of events which occurred. Shortly after Marian's death, I smashed up my car nearly killing myself. The brakes failed for no apparent reason.

"My business, which I had built from nothing into a thriving success, went steadily downward. I had one bad break after another – a fire, unscrupulous wholesalers, until I had to declare bankruptcy.

"I tried to sell the bed," she said nervously, "but as soon as people saw it, they became frightened.

"I tried giving it away. So help me!… A junk dealer took it. The next morning my bed was lying against the side of the apartment building.

"Finally a friend said he was going to prove that this nonsense was all in my head. We took the bed to his place and reconstructed it. But while doing so, a curious thing occurred. As we were putting it together, I was seized by an irresistible impulse and started hammering uncontrollably at the bed, as though it were alive. I wanted to destroy it! My friend looked at me and we began to laugh. He said: 'Did you expect the bed to cry out?'

"We were still laughing when I glanced at the bed, and saw something that stopped me cold. Trickling from the hammer marks were little streams of water, as if the bed was crying.

"I was horror stricken! My friend said – trying to calm hysteria – that it was probably due to condensation from the pipes above. But the bed wasn't anywhere near those pipes!

"A week later my friend came over and said: 'There's no way I'm keeping that bed!' In only seven days, his successful marina business folded after an uncanny series of accidents! He too, accused the bed of laughing.

"I wasn't in it for an hour when it started vibrating … trembling – or something,' he said. 'I didn't believe I'd ever here myself say this, but the thing seemed to be laughing at me!'

"Self-developing photos were taken by a reporter who was going to write a story, but he mysteriously quit his job and has since moved to another part of the country.

"The three photos are still in my possession. The first looks fairly normal. The second has an eerie, glowing light around the periphery of the bed itself, but the third is the weirdest. When he took that picture the first thing we saw was the distinct face of a skull!… Then the bed began to form around it.

"I took my photos and went to see a Toronto psychic, Betty Robinson. She floored me immediately by saying: 'You're terribly worried, and it's over a piece of furniture. Am I right? In fact, I'm sure it's a bed. But there are very bad vibrations around it. It seems a man was poisoned in it and died an agonizing death. Is this correct?' I stuttered, 'I… I don't know.'

"I offered my photos as evidence but she refused to look at them. As I left she told me to get rid of that bed: 'Burn it if necessary.'

"I went home determined to do just that. Burn it! However, no sooner had I arrived home than my daughter announced: 'A mister Terry Filion called, Mother. He's heard about the bed and wants to buy it.'

"As it turned out, Mr. Filion was a dealer and connoisseur of fine old furniture who took one look at the bed and said: 'It's gorgeous. I must have it!' I told him the grisly story, but he insisted on taking the bed immediately.

"My nightmare had ended. I felt as though a great burden had been lifted from my shoulders. But perhaps I should have left well enough alone and not told anyone else this story. Maybe, just maybe, my life and that bed will be intertwined once again…"

The inheritor of Mrs. Milne's bed, the one that brought her so much bad fortune, was ecstatic with his new objet d'art.

In fact, Terry Filion, is now on the highest good luck roll of his life. At least that's what the then 36-year-old music agent was telling people shortly after he purchased the bed. "I just can't believe it – everything is going so right," Terry said."My agency business has literally doubled."I've been in the business 22 years now. And if you now anything about it – I'm into booking one-nighters at clubs and things like that – this is supposed to be a notoriously slow time of this year."But," he added of his company, Canadian General Artists, "We've picked up 20 clubs recently.

"Since I got the bed, I've gone from depression – I'd been considering giving up the agency – to all this… and it's right out of the

Terry Fillion

blue."Other good happened to him too.

He said he had never acted in anything in his life prior to buying the bed, but – just like that – he got roles in three movies shot in the Toronto area, including two with Peter O'Toole and Mickey Rooney. "It's unreal… I ran into Henry Fonda (who was also filming in the Toronto area) totally by accident, and he gave me a number to call, and that was it for one film."

Fillion had not yet slept in the bed, though. "But I will, sure," he said, "bad luck won't happen to me."

Part 2

Fillion gave a party at his Scarborough home the day that he bought the bed.

Around 8 p.m. the guests began to arrive and by 10 his party was in full swing. Terry was having a drink with some friends when Laura Hamilton, a dark-haired woman who owns a boutique, approached him. Laura was determined to see the bed that she had heard so much about.

"We went to the room where I kept the bed," Filion told me, "When Laura saw it her eyes widened like a child with a new toy. The woman squealed with delight as her fingers moved along the wood. But when she touched the emblem at the top of the headboard, she quickly withdrew her hands while a strange silence fell over her.

"I asked what was wrong. She said after touching the bat figure on the headboard, a weird sensation went through her, like an electric shock.

"I told her to stop being silly and not to let some ridiculous story frighten her. Just then she began shivering, and her face turned a deathly white. Concerned about her distress, I intimated: 'Perhaps you've had too much to drink?'

"'No, but please, just get me out of here," was her response.

"A week later the phone rang. It was Laura. I could hardly recognize her voice – she was so hysterical! She wanted to come over right away.

"Laura ran through my front door screaming that the bed had done something to her. I was shocked by her appearance, the woman looked terrible!

"Laura actually believed that something had taken possession of her, and she begged me to help her!

"We went into the room, but I was totally unprepared for what followed. I have to say here and now that I'm a businessman who will only accept what can be seen and touched – but what I say, my mind still can't accept…

"Laura stood by the top of my bed, and I was near the foot. I really had no idea of what to do, but I held onto the bottom bedpost with my left hand, while my right held Laura's left arm. She touched the bat emblem with her free hand. Then all hell broke loose.

"Suddenly Laura's eyes rolled back and she went into convulsions: Her body shook violently – and, so help me, a spark leapt from the top of the bed, went through her body and snapped my arm with such force, that I later had my doctor examine it.

"When Laura came to," Terry continued, "she seemed perfectly normal and unharmed but, more extraordinarily, spoke of a message for me sent by whoever or whatever controlled that bed! I know this sounds unbelievable, but the purported message is: 'I was a man… I will not harm you… I need your help…'

"Then she went home. A day later I received a call from the hospital. Laura had become violently ill during the night and was rushed to emergency. I was shocked!"

Terry Filion's story sound incredible, even bizarre. But from a hospital sick-bed, Laura Hamilton of Weston, Ontario, tells her version of what occurred that night.

"Well, when we got to the party, I walked up to Mr. Filion and demanded to see he bed I had heard so much about.

"I was really taking the whole thing as a lark. Everything was fine until I touched it – especially the bat emblem! All at once my head began to swim and I felt nauseous, then I blacked out, or so Mr. Filion says.

"Anyway, after coming to I left as fast as possible. Even quicker. I was petrified! All through the night I tossed and turned. Sleep will not come. When it did, it became a nightmare. When morning came I literally dragged myself to the shop. All day I was ill, continually bringing up.

Terry Fillion with Headboard

"Still sick, I went home and straight to my room. My mother kept insisting that I come down for dinner. Then, for no apparent reason I flew into a rage – picked up a heavy book-end and hurled it at my mother's head! Thank God it missed, it would have killed her. As if that wasn't bad enough, then I lunged at her! My father grabbed me just in time. I don't know what would have happened if he hadn't.

"I ran out of the house and went to see Mr. Filion screaming that the bed had cursed me. After I left there and got back home I became violently ill and... here we are. The doctors still don't know what's wrong. But I do. Somehow, that bed is responsible."

Christine Easson of Toronto, Ontario, owns a custom made furniture and interior decorating business, House of Lenne.

In an interview, Ms. Easson told me this: "Mr. Filion brought in this bed to be refinished. It was a very busy day, so the workman put it in the far corner of the warehouse, and we promptly forgot about it.

"All that week people were complaining – wrong wallpaper, wrong colors cancel this, cancel that. My nerves were at the breaking point. What had I done wrong?

"On Friday afternoon three of my workers were preparing to deliver a very valuable, delicate glass cocktail table. It shattered, just like that, for no apparent reason." However, I got into my car that Friday evening but, it wouldn't start. The mechanic was going

Christine Easson

to be a while, so I began walking around the factory. All at once my eyes fell upon it, the bed! I had completely forgotten. In a flash, it dawned on me; could there be any truth to that myth?

"I timidly approached it and touched that bat thing on the headboard. A grayish mist slowly oozed from that figurehead. I screamed.

"The next morning I sent for the very best craftsmen to come in and do the refinishing.

"I wanted that thing removed – quickly. These people are expert European artisans. They completed the job and my workmen had instructions to send it back that evening.

"At six p.m., my secretary came and told me the job had not been properly done, there were water stains all over the bed, plus the lacquer was dissipating.

"I could hardly believe it, but it was true!

"The company sent the craftsmen back, and once again they worked on it. These men are extremely good at their work, and they said this was the first time they had to do a job over again.

"The foreman said the apparent bleeding, or crying of the wood, was virtually impossible because of the way it was kiln dried.

"As soon as they finished, I sent it back. Later, Mr. Filion phoned and told me the tear-stains were back and that it looked as though it hadn't even been touched!

"I'm a very religious woman, so I got myself a crucifix. I feel a great need for one."

Frank Kard of Toronto owns what is supposedly the mate to Filion's bed. The claim is that the last person to die in Terry's haunted bed was a man, has been supported by a host of psychics. With that in mind, here then is Kard's story.

"My wife is an antique buff," Kard told me, "one day she came home all excited and told me she had found just the bed we were looking for. We brought this bed home over two years ago, and have never slept in it. Why? I'll tell you…

"The night we put up the bed, my wife went to a fortune teller with a few of her friends. This fellow, Mr. Irving, was so uncannily accurate that, according to my wife, he talked about my past life as if he were reading a book, and even predicted my present career.

"But then he said something that was a trifle unnerving, especially since he was so accurate on every other point. He told my wife that she had just purchased an old bed, but not to sleep in it or keep it around.

"He told her the bed was surrounded by bad vibrations – or whatever these

Bill Rogers

people call it. He also said, and get this, that there was a mate to my bed which was especially unlucky for women, because it was possessed by a spirit of a man who had been poisoned by his wife and then died in it; and that it (the other bed) has been associated with much evil over many years. Finally," Kard continued, "Irving ended by telling her that both beds came from the part of Europe known as Transylvania."

The haunted bed was put on a display at a fair in London, Ontario. This exhibition also played host to a psychic convention, so the bed was minutely examined by a raft of sensitives.

Possessed, evil, demonic: On and on it went until over 30 self-acclaimed psychics had investigated this phenomenon, each giving the same negative reading.

Bill Rogers, a reporter and newscaster from Toronto radio station CKFM, photographed the bed. His comment? "I snapped three Polaroid shots," Bill told me, "the first two, as they developed, formed the face of a man with straight black hair. After the picture had completely developed, the apparition disappeared into the background.

"The third photo, which was the strangest, appeared to have long spear-like sparks shooting out from the bed! I must confess, I find it very strange. Even frightening. I've never seen anything quite like it...

Part 3

From the beginning I was warned not to get involved. Betty Robinson advised me to stay away from the bed. Norman Johnston, another psychic, said: 'I'm not so sure this is a good idea, Tony, Maybe you should give it up.' When I saw Eileen Sonin, yet another psychic, she warned me: 'If I was you, I would get away from that bed as soon as possible.'

I should have known better than to laugh, after reading the hands of so many unpredictable and bizarre people, and the mysteries with which I've been involved.

That past year I had an incredible run of luck... all bad. I was the worst I have ever experienced.

On the eve of the first part of the bed story being published I was having dinner in a restaurant when I suddenly stopped talking and clutched my throat. The most excruciating pain was tearing through it.

At St. Michael's Hospital tests revealed nothing organic. The doctors dragged out that old stock reading: 'It's just your nerves, my boy.'

A few days later the pain subsided a little, but for the next 13 months a strangling sensation was my constant companion.

You see, I'm also a saxophone player or rather – I was, before this happened. Blowing a horn isn't comfortable at the best of times, much less when one is suffering exquisite pain.

A week later, right on the street, another attack followed. I got into a cab and went to the nearest hospital. They examined me and found nothing. What was causing it? Suspicions about the bed began seeping into my mind.

Unfortunate incidents occurred in rapid succession. Several TV stations had been extremely interested in my scripts. The talks collapsed.

My articles ceased being published. Fear began to set in... maybe this bed was responsible for my bad luck. Money was low; so like many people whose business or career was slipping away, I started drinking. And I mean drinking; the pressure on my throat was relentless.

Desperate, I accepted a playing job in a little northern town. An hour after starting work I was in the emergency room. The pain was unbearable. Morphine had to be used.

All tests and examinations proved negative. They kept me overnight. In the morning the specialist told me he was baffled. The specialist in Toronto gave me the full treatment – isotopes, x-rays; he probed, prodded, squeezed and arrived at the same negative diagnosis. After that, things started going bad.

On November 1 of 1978, my former wife was nearly killed in a car accident. Her face will never be the same. On November 17, a girl who was driving my car ran it into a parked truck. I was a passenger and it's a miracle we weren't killed.

As if that wasn't enough, the same night while walking from the police station to a cab I fell and sprained my hip – and I was cold sober.

Something was desperately wrong. A year ago everything was coming up roses, and now…? Once again I contacted Filion.

During the past year Terry claimed only good luck since he had bought the bed. But later he admitted to an unfortunate series of events.

At first he blamed an anti-Christ plaque given to him by Bob Gallo of CBS Records. Terry thought it may have acted as a catalyst when it was placed between him and the bed, which he kept in his office. Blaming the bed, Terry had given the bed to some acquaintances who were moving to the U.S.

He told me: "…They were a married couple with a six-year-old daughter. There mother had expressed an inordinate interest in the bed. When they told me they were leaving, I agreed to let them have it.

"Several weeks later two detectives came to my door. They said that my friend had reported his wife missing for over a week.

"A month later, police charged him with murder. My friend – this man whom I had known for years, and who was always a quiet person, went berserk and strangled her." "He stuffed the body into a white, porcelain barrel and sealed it behind a brick wall. The real tragedy is the child. She witnessed everything.

The police said, according to the child's testimony, that she was murdered in my bed! I was horrified but at the same time fascinated."

The bed was then returned back to Toronto.

Countess Helena de Silaghi is an author, a psychic and an internationally acclaimed artist who lives near Toronto. Yet she's famous for something else. The countess claims descent from Vlad the Impaler, better known as Count Dracula!

Yes, he really existed, and so did Transylvaniam high in the Carpathian Mountains of Eastern Europe. Countess de Silaghi was born in Turda-Cluj, Transylvania, and her family has lived the since the eighth century.

I went to the countess, and after examining photos of the bed with a magnifying glass, she said in her heavy Romanian accent: 'This bed comes from my country. The bat-figure on the headboard is a familiar emblem.'

"Is there anything to this ghost stuff?" I asked. She said: "We each have three bodies, which ecclesiastics refer to as 'the father, the son and the holy ghost.'

"I call the physical, ectoplasmic and ethereal bodies. The ectoplasmic, or middle body, acts like a lubricant allowing the physical and ethereal bodies to function smoothly."

"Ectoplasm is basically physical, and therefore confined to our Earth plane. When natural death occurs, a process takes place comparable to a three stage rocket. The ectoplasmic body leaves the physical, the ethereal leaves the ectoplasmic and goes on to the next plane.

"However, if the mediate body is damaged, as by violent death, then the spirit wanders the earth until the outer layer disintegrates allowing the ethereal entity to escape. This may take from a few years to several hundred. Hence, you have your spectres, poltergeists, etc."

The countess continued: "There is nothing more personal than a bed. People are born, make love and die in a bed.

"I'm sure there are spirits – probably more than one – surrounding, but not infused throughout, the wood. Each time this object is moved, the troubled souls who in life were associated with the bed are terribly upset. This, my friend, will create negative vibrations."

I thanked her and left to interview Bob Gallo. And when I met him I was astounded by his resemblance to popular caricatures of Satan.

He confirmed what the countess had told me. "Do you feel there's a tie-in between Filion's bed and your association with him?" I asked.

"You know," he said, "when I first saw that bed it was just another piece of furniture. But since then so many unusual things have occurred."

As I turned to leave my eye caught sight of a wall painting. My jaw dropped when I read the signature. It was signed …de Silaghi.

"How long has this been here, Mr. Gallo?"

"About six years. Why?"

I left without answering. It was December 20, and outside sleet was falling. I asked the receptionist to call a cab. She tried in vain. By now the streets were glazed with ice. Gay Gennings, Gallo's secretary, walked by and suggested that if I drove her car she would give me a lift. I agreed.

I carefully drove through the traffic snarls, but as our car approached a steep hill terminating at Lake Ontario, someone or something pulled the rug from under us.

We started sliding, and my last words to Gay were: "One thing I can promise you, this definitely won't be boring."

The first car I hit went flying down ahead of us. Then we bounced off another vehicle parked on the opposite side; it too slipped away. They say everything happens in threes, so we spun our way back to the original curb and, yes, even hit a third car, which also went to the bottom of the hill.

There is a happy ending, though. The three vehicles provided a cushion for us, and our smashing into them prevented us from sliding further, perhaps even into the lake.

And while I really hate to complain, gee, I have seen better years.

Whatever happens, I'm sure we haven't heard the last of the bed; and I've gained a very healthy respect for it.

Betty Robinson says "Burn it!" I agree. But who will strike the first match?

THIS BOOK FEATURES

"THE WORLD'S MOST DOCUMENTED PSYCHIC!"

HIS PREDICTIONS FOR THE COMING MILLENIUM...

A FEW OF HIS FULFILLED PREDICTIONS INCLUDE:

THE 9/11 TERRORIST ATTACK!

ACTOR ROBERT BLAKE'S ACQUITTAL OF WIFE'S MURDER!

YASSER ARAFAT'S SUDDEN AND MYSTERIOUS DEATH!

ANTHONY CARR

"An important and timely book...A must read!"
Allen Spraggett, AUTHOR OF "THE UNEXPLAINED" AND 14 OTHER BOOKS ON THE PARANORMAL

"Scandalous!...Sex! Politics! Hollywood! It's all here!"
Joe Mullins, MANAGING EDITOR, GLOBE MAGAZINE

"The book knocked me out!"
Sylvester Stallone, HOLLYWOOD STAR

"A haunting story, well told."
Les Pyette, PUBLISHER AND CEO SUN NEWSPAPERS

Anthony Carr's predictions and palm readings are often featured
in The Star, Globe, Enquirer, The National Examiner, The Sun and
other newspapers and magazines.

He has also appeared on all the major talk shows including
Howard Stern, the Daily Show (with John Stewart), The Rosanne
Show, The David Brenner and many, many more.

$ 9.95 U.S.

$ 12.95 Cdn

<u>Nostradamus</u>

From the Complete Prophecies of Nostradamus. By Henry C. Roberts: First published 1947, last published 1975

*Note: Any references to the "new-world" or the "new city" refers to "America," since during most of his prophecies were made circa 1555 - shortly after Christopher Columbus discovered the New-World - America! **(Anthony Carr)**

New York twin towers catastrophe!!!

Quatrain 97, p. 211: "The heaven shall burn at five and forty degrees. The fire shall come near the great 'new city!' In an instant a great flame dispersed shall burst out, When they shall make a trail of the Normans."

Interpretation: "A cataclysmic fire shall engulf the greatest and 'newest' of the world's big cities." New York City is exactly at forty-five degrees latitude! -- plus, both planes hit the buildings at approximately 45 degrees latitude! **(Anthony Carr)**

The attack on New York City

Quatrain 87, p. 37: "Ennosige, fire of the center of the earth, Shall make an earthquake of the New City, Two great rocks (World Trade Centers?) shall long time war against each other, after that, Arethusa shall colour red the fresh river."

Interpretation: "A terrific fire, of the same nature as that at the center of the earth, shall make a shambles of 'New___ City.'" Arethusa was an ever flowing classic spring. **(Anthony Carr)**

The attack on New York City

Quatrain 190, p. 144: "Fire shall fall from the skies on the King's palace (World Trade Centers?) When Mar's light shall be eclipsed, Great War shall be for seven months, people shall die by witchcraft, Rouen and Eureux shall not fail the King."

Interpretation: "A seven month's war, of tremendous destructive force such as the world has never seen before shall terrify man kind!" **(Anthony Carr)**

Second attack on America
Quatrain 23, p. 118: "The Legion in the Maritime Fleet, Calcening greatly, shall burn brimstone and pitch, after a long rest in the secure place (America, fifty-seven relatively peaceful years since end of WW II), They shall seek Port Selyn, but fire shall consume them."
Interpretation: "A terrific assault by a great fleet equipped with weapons employing potent chemical agents (Anthrax, etc.) shall attack a country which has long enjoyed peace and security (America). They shall attack the great Port of Les N.Y. but will be repulsed (by America) by weapons even more terrible!" (Anthony Carr)

Attack on America (New York)
Quatrain 72, p. 336: "In the year 1999 and seven months, From the skies shall come an invasion, a 'war of the worlds,' to raise again the powerful and mighty King of Jacquerie (King of the peasants), Before and after, Mars (war) shall reign at will!"
Interpretation: "I'm certain this refers to the attack on New York and the Pentagon. Although Nostradamus was off by two years, I stated at the time that this event will occur even though the predicted date has passed. And, we may yet face an invasion from another world...Only time will tell."
"A tremendous world revolution is foretold to take place in the year 1999 (2001), with a complete upheaval of existing social orders, preceded by world-wide wars, followed by an epoch of peace, a Uni-religion and One world leader, who restores and keeps the peace." (Anthony Carr)

Osama bin Laden, the Antichrist, and the Armageddon predictions.
Quotes from: Nostradamus: Countdown to Apocalypse, by John Charles de Fontbryne.
"Soiled by murders and abominable crimes, this great enemy of the human race will be worse than all his predecessors! By the sword and flame of war he will shed blood in inhuman fashion!"
 (P.421, CX,Q10)

"The Antichrist will soon annihilate three countries. The war he will wage will last twenty-seven years. Opponents will be put to death and prisoners deported. Blood from bodies will redden the water, the land will be riddled with blows (missiles, bombardments)."   (P.423, CVIII, Q17)

"The airborne invasion of New York in July, 1999 (September 11, 2001) a great and terrifying leader will come through the skies to revive (the memory of) the great conqueror Angoulême. Before and after, war will rule luckily."   (Cx, 972)
Interpretation: "Obviously, New York City." (Anthony Carr)

Powerful enemy hidden within bosom of New York City.
Quatrain 92, p.308: "The King shall desire to enter into the 'New City.' With foes they shall come to overcome it, The prisoner being freed, shall speak and act falsely, The King being gotten out, shall keep far from enemies."
Interpretation: "The 'New City' (New York?) shall be besieged by a powerful person, helped by spies within!"
(Anthony Carr)

A tidal wave of putrid water throughout New York, New Jersey or Atlantic City
Quatrain 49, p. 328: "Garden of the World (Garden State?), near the New City (New York?), in the way of the Man-made mountains (Skyscrapers?), Shall be seized on and plunged into a ferment (putrid), Being forced to drink sulphurous poisoned waters."
Interpretation: "This startling prophecy of a catastrophic event at a pleasure resort not far from the great 'new city,' predicts a tremendous tidal wave of poisoned waters that shall sweep in from 'the resort' and overwhelm the man-made mountain-like skyscrapers of the city."
(Anthony Carr)

One religion - for all!
Quatrain 72, p. 302: "Once more shall the Holy Temple be polluted, And depredated by the Senate of Toulouse, Saturn two, .

three cycles revolving, In April, May, people of a new heaven."
Interpretation: "According to this prophecy, there will be a
complete revision of the basic concepts of religion about the year
2150 (600 years after it was written), and a 'new-world' (America?)
Order will arise" (possibly one religion for all!).
(Anthony Carr)

Terrible war, followed by a 'new-world' leader who will initiate a
long peace
Quatrain 24, p. 187: "Mars and the Secptre, being conjoined
together, Under Cancer shall be a calamitous war, A little while after
a new King shall be anointed, Who, for a long time, shall pacify the
earth."
Interpretation: "Nostradamus here speaks of a constellation called
the Sceptre. Looking at what was then the far future (1555), he
foretells of a time when this constellation shall be in conjunction
with Mars, and the terrible war that will break out under this
influence. And out of the debacle there will arise a "new-world"
leader ("new-world," United States President?) and peace will reign
for a long time afterward."
(Anthony Carr)

Quatrain 70, p. 202: "A chief of the world, the great Henry shall be,
at first, beloved, afterwards feared, dreaded, His fame and praise
shall go beyond the heavens! And shall be contented with the title
of Victor."
Interpretation: "The nations will organize a super-government
covering the entire world! The president will be called, or
named, Henry. "Chryen' by transposition of letters is an anagram
for "Henry,' then current form of Henry."
(Anthony Carr)

Eventual world peace (egalitarianism)
Quatrain 10, p. 182: "Within a little while the temples of the
colors, White and black shall be intermixed, red and yellow shall
take away their colors, Blood, earth, plague, famine, fire, water shall
destroy them."

Interpretation: "After a period of much travail all the races of the world shall lose their prejudices and be as one."
(Anthony Carr)

Quatrain 89, pg. 341: "The walls shall be turned from brick into marble, There shall be peace for seven and fifty years, Joy to mankind; the aqueduct shall be rebuilt, Health, abundance of fruits, joys and a mellifluous time."
Interpretation: "Nostradamus predicts a golden age for humanity after a great calamitous war among nations. *Personally, I think this refers to the end of World War II till the present — exactly fifty seven years (1945-2002), then hostilities begin anew!"
(Anthony Carr)

Yet another prediction of eventual world peace
Quatrain 66, p. 300: "Peace, union, shall be and profound changes, Estates, offices, the low high and the high very low A journey shall be prepared for, the first fruit, pains, War shall cease, also civil processes and strife."
Interpretation:"A Utopian age shall come into being in the course of time, but not without pain."
Quatrain 96, p. 344:   "Religion of the name of the seas shall come, Against the Sect of 'Caitif of the Moon,' The deplorably obstinate sect, shall be afraid, Of the two wounded by A. and A."
Interpretation: "One must delve deeply into these cryptic words in order to grasp their full meaning.   The 'Caitifs of the Moon' indicates the Arab nation. The phrase "A. and A." means America. The sense, then, is that there will be a struggle between the opposing philosophies of the two groups." (*To say the least — hindsight!)
Now we can see it: "Religion of the name of the seas shall come, against the 'Sect of Caitifs of the Moon' (Arab Nations flag is the quarter-moon and star; the word
'Caitif' in the Unabridged Oxford Dictionary means: base,cowardly and despicable), the deplorably obstinate sect shall be afraid of the two wounded by A. and A. This sneaky, cowardly murderous people shall become afraid of, then destroyed by, A. and A. - America!!! (Anthony Carr)

The sudden end of global war!
Quatrain 53, p. 162: "The law of Sun and Venus contending, appropriating the spirit of prophecy, Neither one nor the other shall

be heard, By Sol the law of the great Messiah shall subsist."
Interpretation: "The forces of light and darkness, struggling for domination over the spirit of man, shall both be superseded by the new law of the great Saviour!" (*Or, if I may suggest, "The Great and Mighty One will halt the carnage, lest all flesh perish!...Supreme Star-traveller, or God, who created us all — Christian, Muslim and Jew.)
(Anthony Carr)

Quatrain 99, p. 345: "At last the wolf, the lion, ox and ass, The gentle doe, shall be down with mastiffs. The manna shall no more fall to them, There shall be no more watching and keeping of mastiffs."
Interpretation: "This reiterates previous Prognostications of a period of peace and plenty, and of elimination of war."
And peace!!! Anthony Carr

priesthood, *when suddenly - without warning; the book flew out of my hands and landed at my feet - upside down!*

I saw immediately from this angle that the picture of the insect was quite different - it actually portrayed very clearly the image of a gigantic spacecraft landing in a blaze of fire and smoke. This revelation was the beginning of my lifelong commitment to the idea that The Star Traveler / Lord of Lords had visited the earth in ancient time and his appearance is revealed in the images of pagan literature, as well as The Bible.

The Scarab Beetle has long been regarded as an ancient Egyptian symbol of myth and magic.

But is it a beetle?

What would a dung beetle have to do with reverence and mysticism? Perhaps it is not a beetle at *all!*

For five thousand years we have been looking at this picture from the wrong angle. Turn it upside down and you will see an amazing image - that of a magnificent **Space Craft** which is landing (or blasting off) in an explosion of light and flames!

Now we can see why this image, when viewed from the **proper perspective**, was held in such reverence and high regard by The Ancients!

The mystical, magical **Scarab Beetle of Egypt** was for thousands of years an object of reverence but people have been looking at it *upside down!*

Not This Way...

Photograph of an ancient Egyptian religious artifact which clearly shows the image of the **Sacred Scarab Beetle.**

Anthony Carr

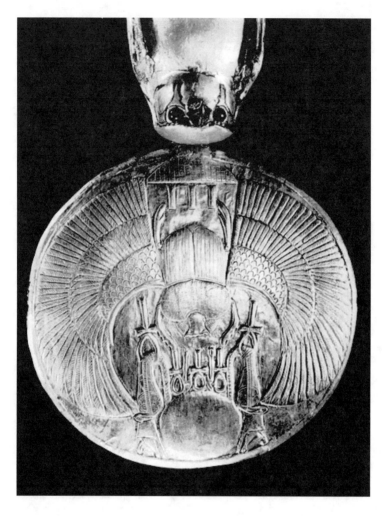

...But this way!

Can you see the spaceship?

Was God a Star Traveler?

A passage from The Bible which describes the landing of a huge spacecraft. God in the form of The Star Traveler helps David defeat his enemies.

From Psalm 18:

"In my distress I called upon The Lord for help." *...David is in trouble. He communicates to his protector who is **The Star Traveler** on Mount Sinai.*

"From his temple (the UFO) he heard my voice, and I am saved from my enemies." *...message received and understood.* "He rode on a cherub, and flew; He came swiftly upon the wings of the wind.

"Then The Earth reeled and rocked; the foundations also of the mountains trembled and quaked because He was angry"... *the powerful engines of the spacecraft cause earthquake-like reverberations throughout the immediate area.*

"Then smoke went up from his nostrils (emissions from the rocket exhausts) and devouring fire from his mouth: glowing coals flamed forth from Him." ... *the heat from the engines burns the grasses, shrubs and kindles stones; it becomes so intense as the engines accelerate, that small rocks in the vicinity of the thrusting, blasting rockets begin to ignite.*

"He smote my enemies with arrows of lightning." ... *laser rays from the UFO's?*

"The Lord also thundered in the heavens and The Most High uttered his voice at the blast of the breath of thy nostrils." ... *the craft rumbled, roared and accelerated overhead.*

Religion

We are Living in the Beginning Days of the Coming Tribulation.

By: Anthony Carr

A mighty sign in the heavens shall apprise us of the Great One's return. (Star-Traveler, Lord of Lords, King of Kings!)

From the sky Gods you will hear and know everything. I predict Eternal God shall tread upon the Earth and on that day all shall be smitten with fear and trembling—even unto the ends of the earth!

Terrible upheavals! The high mountains shall be shaken, the high hills made low; (nearly) all that is upon the earth shall perish, and there shall be a Judgment on every man (and woman).

Truly the kind and the righteous He shall save and protect. But not the hypocrites!

There is soon to be another pandemic Cosmic shock to our collective Psyche, which must occur to modify man's violent behaviour, to put back the fear of God in us. And soon!

The Antichrist will rise out of Africa, evil as black as his heart. To the dark place shall shift the turmoil. He tears the world apart. Once, twice, removed from the East! —the sojourn hails his new start. (P.S. We will all recognize him as being from the past.)

But first, behold! He cometh with ten thousand times ten thousand of His holy ones (astronauts), to execute Judgment upon all and to destroy the ungodly!

Then the angels (extraterrestrial astronauts), the children of heaven, will once again lust after the daughters of men, and take unto themselves from among them, wives.
Then shall He make peace with the Elect, and they shall prosper.

But before the Peace, a great destruction shall be wrought upon the earth, and men shall know agony for five months and three days; he shall see the destruction of his children, and all whom he loves, over and over again, but mercy and peace shall he not attain.

Then a great light shall descend from heaven, coming down

like a brilliant, many-colored jewel, and the King of Kings shall step forward to save the world, less all perish! (i.e., Commander in Chief of astronauts, head Honcho—etc...) So sparkling will be his raiment that all the inhabitants of the world will not look upon it directly.

Then shall the Great and Glorious One sit upon his earthly throne thereon. And his raiment more bright than the sun and all the stars shall hold the children of earth in awe, and He shall judge the world.... (From the Ancient Book of Enoch, with commentary by Anthony Carr)

"In God's high place above the world and the firmament, I proceeded to where everything was chaotic and horrible: I saw neither heaven alone nor a firmly founded earth but a place terrible and awful! And it was burning with fire. And I asked the angel (astronaut): 'For what sin are they bound and on what account have they been cast in hither?'

"Then said Uriel, the angel of the Lord, said unto me: 'why dost thou ask, and why art thou eager for the truth? These souls have transgressed the commandment of the Lord and are bound here till ten thousand years, the time allotted for their sins, are consummated'

"And from thence, I went to another place, which was more terrible than the former, and I saw a horrible thing: a great fire there which burnt and blazed!
"Then I said: 'How fearful is this place and how terrible to look upon!' Then Uriel answered me, and said: 'Enoch, why hast though such fear and affright?' And I answered, 'Because of this fearful place, and because of the spectacle of the pain!'
"And he said unto me: 'This place is the prison of the (evil) angels, and here they will be imprisoned forever!' (In this terrible and chaotic corner of the Universe—hell! Yet the good angels -- "Souls" -- shall bask in the soft light of God's Eternal heaven.)
"Then Uriel said unto me: 'Here their spirits shall be set apart (in heaven and hell) till the great day of Judgment, and the punishment and torment of those who curse forever, and the retribution for their sins, and for even the false Christendom" (the false church).
His Judgment cometh and that right soon: The cities like unto Sodom and Gomorrah shall be destroyed first, at the outbreak of

Armageddon.

"And there, above the earth and the firmament, I came face to face with the King of Heaven, the God of Glory ("Glory" means bright light), and mine eyes saw the secrets of the lightning's, and the lights, and the peels of thunder by which the Lord executed his command."

(Probably aboard a UFO, Enoch was bedazzled and bewildered by the maze of flashing colored lights and booming loudspeakers through which orders were barked. Remember: this is a primitive cave dweller, completely ignorant of electricity—or superior energy power—and all of its multi-faceted uses.)

"I alone have seen this vision, the end of all things, and no man shall see as I have seen." From "The Ancient Book of Enoch"

The Beautiful Story of Christmas

A modern interpretation, of course, by Anthony Carr.

I have always believed that the star of Bethlehem was a UFO, which led the three Magi to the Christ child. That Mary was put into a deep sleep by the Archangel/Star-Traveler Gabriel and, through some form of extra-terrestrial artificial insemination, impregnated her and — viola! — a superior human being, who was and was not of this world, was conceived (the virgin birth); and the angel of the Lord who appeared to the shepherds "watching over their flocks by night" was most certainly an extraterrestrial astronaut.

A theory that his resurrection could have been the result of the cloning of his own body's DNA, and his "ascension into heaven," perhaps to the Mother ship and head-Honcho Star-Traveller, a sort of a "Beam me up, Scotty!" will be proffered by someone other than me (for a change), a respected member of the scientific community.

Thus we have the beautiful story of Christmas:

"And God (the "good" Star-Traveller) sent the angel Gabriel (one of his astronauts) to a city of Galilee named Nazareth, to a virgin named Mary who was betrothed to a man called Joseph; and the angel appeared to her, and said, 'Hail, O favored one, the Lord is with you! Do not be afraid, Mary, for you have found favor with God.'

'And behold, you will conceive in your womb and bear a son, and you shall call his name Jesus. He will be great, and will be called the Son of the Most High; and the Lord God will give to him the throne

of his father, David, and of his kingdom there will be no end; and he will reign over the house of Jacob forever.'

"And Mary said to the angel, 'How shall this be, since I have no husband?' And the angel said to her, 'The Holy Spirit will come upon you (advanced technical type of impregnation) and the power of the Most High will overshadow you; therefore, the child to be born will be called Holy, the Son of God.' (Luke 1:26-35)

"And there were shepherds out in the field keeping watch over their flocks by night. (Again) an angel of the Lord appeared to them and the glory (very bright lights) of the Lord shone around them, and they were filled with fear." (Throughout the Bible whenever 'the glory of the Lord' is mentioned it always pertains to brightly shining lights which, centuries before the advent of electricity, certainly would seem like a 'glorious' miracle, indeed.)

"And the angel said to them, 'Be not afraid; for behold, I bring you good tidings of great joy which shall be to all men; for to you is born this day in the city of David a Saviour, who is Christ the Lord. And this will be a sign unto you; you will find a babe wrapped in swaddling clothes and lying in a manger.'

"And suddenly there was with the angel a multitude of the heavenly host (many celestial astronauts with either oxygen tanks or levitating devices on their backs, often depicted in Christian religion paintings as 'wings' — who were frolicking to and fro), praising God and saying, 'Glory to God in the highest, and on Earth, peace and goodwill toward men with whom he is pleased!' When the angels went away from them into heaven," etc.... (Luke 2:8-15)

And then there were the three wise men who followed the star of Bethlehem, a very brilliantly lit UFO: "And lo, the star which they had seen in the east went before them (that is, led them, till it came to rest, or stop) over the place where the child was."

The Old and New Testaments are rife with stories about Star-Travelers, e.g., when Moses brought the people of Israel up to Mt. Sinai:

"Thus the Lord used to speak to Moses, face to face, as a man

speaks to his friend." (Exodus 33:11)
And as well: Psalm 18 is strongly descriptive of a UFO (unidentified
flying object):
    "In my distress I called upon the Lord for help." (David is
in trouble, so he communicates with his protector, the Star-Traveler,
on Mt. Sinai): "From his temple (the UFO) he heard my voice, and
I am saved from my enemies." (Message received and understood.)
"Then the earth reeled and rocked; the foundations also of the
mountains trembled and quaked because he was angry" (The
powerful engines of a rocket or space craft cause earthquake-like
reverberations throughout the immediate area.) "Then smoke went
up from his nostrils (emissions from the rocket exhausts), and
devouring fire from his mouth; glowing coals flamed forth from
him." (The heat from the engines burns the grasses, shrubs and
kindles stones; it becomes so intense, as the engines accelerate, that
small rocks in the vicinity of the thrusting, blasting rockets begin to
ignite.) "He smote mine enemies with arrows of lightning. (Laser
rays from the UFO's?)
"The Lord also thundered in the heavens, and the Most High
uttered his voice at the blast of the breath of thy nostrils." (The craft
rumbled, roared and accelerated overhead. It's no wonder David
spent so much time singing praises to the Lord, or Star-Traveler, he
would have been a dead duck without him.)

The lovely story of Easter:
"Now after the Sabbath, toward the dawn of the first day of the
week, Mary Magdalene and the other Mary went to the sepulchre.
And behold, there was a great earthquake (hovering space craft
causing the ground to tremble?); for an angel (astronaut) of the Lord
(head Honcho Star-Traveler?) descended from heaven and came
and rolled back the stone, and sat upon it.
"His appearance was like lighting and his raiment white as snow."
(Probably because of his phosphorus-like, or shiny space suit
resembling those that the earth astronauts wore during the 1969
moon landing.)
Mathew 8:1-20
Watch the heavens for the return of the Star-Travelers, who will

intervene in the affairs of Man and halt the violence: "And I saw the holy city (gloriously brilliant UFO), new Jerusalem, coming down out of the heaven from God, prepared as a bride adorned for her husband; having the glory of God, its radiance like a most rare jewel, a jasper, clear as crystal.

"And I heard a loud voice from the throne saying, "Behold, the dwelling of God is with men. He will dwell with them, and they shall be his people, and God, himself (supreme Star Chief), will be with them;

"He will wipe away every tear from their eyes, and death shall be no more, neither shall there be mourning nor crying nor pain anymore."

Revelation 21:1-4 & 11

Watch! They are coming! And there shall be peace...

THE END – AND THE BEGINNING!

Bald Gorby – Beauty or the Beast?

Anthony Carr, noted psychic and palmist, confronted Gorbachev who was touring Variety Village in Toronto, Canada. Carr believes the mark on Gorby's forehead indicates he could be "The Beast" referred to in Revelation.

"...One of its heads '_seemed_' to have a mortal wound, but its mortal wound was healed..." (Revelation 13:3)

THIS BOOK FEATURES
"THE WORLD'S MOST DOCUMENTED PSYCHIC!"
HIS PREDICTIONS FOR THE COMING MILLENIUM...

A FEW OF HIS FULFILLED PREDICTIONS INCLUDE:

THE 9/11 TERRORIST ATTACK!

ACTOR ROBERT BLAKE'S ACQUITTAL OF WIFE'S MURDER!

YASSER ARAFAT'S SUDDEN AND MYSTERIOUS DEATH!

ANTHONY CARR

"An important and timely book...A must read!"
Allen Spraggett, AUTHOR OF "THE UNEXPLAINED" AND 14 OTHER BOOKS ON THE PARANORMAL

"Scandalous!...Sex! Politics! Hollywood! It's all here!"
Joe Mullins, MANAGING EDITOR, GLOBE MAGAZINE

"The book knocked me out!"
Sylvester Stallone, HOLLYWOOD STAR

"A haunting story, well told."
Les Pyette, PUBLISHER AND CEO SUN NEWSPAPERS

Anthony Carr's predictions and palm readings are often featured
in The Star, Globe, Enquirer, The National Examiner, The Sun and
other newspapers and magazines.

He has also appeared on all the major talk shows including
Howard Stern, the Daily Show (with John Stewart), The Rosanne
Show, The David Brenner and many, many more.

$ 9.95 U.S.

$ 12.95 Cdn